BRISTOL OLD VIC THEATRE SCHOOL

the first 50 years

1946-1996

Shirley Brown

BRISTOL OLD VIC THEATRE SCHOOL *the first 50 years* **1946-1996,** first published in 1996 in the United Kingdom by BOVTS Productions Ltd, 1 & 2 Downside Road, Clifton, Bristol BS8 2XF and distributed by Nick Hern Books, 14 Larden Road, London W3 7ST.

British Library Cataloguing data for this book is available from the British Library.

ISBN 1 85459 395 1

Printed in Great Britain by T O Elworthy & Son Ltd, Bristol.

Shirley Brown is a Bristol-based freelance writer and broadcaster who has provided programme notes for Bristol Old Vic productions since 1987, produced documentaries about the Theatre Royal, the BOV Company and the Theatre School for BBC Radio Bristol, and since 1982 regularly written for Bristol/Bath listings magazine *Venue,* of which she is Theatre Editor. She contributed an essay, *The Bristol Theatre Royal - The Continuing Story 1966-93,* to *Scenes from Provincial Stages,* published in 1994 by The Society for Theatre Research as a tribute to theatre historian Kathleen Barker, author of *The Theatre Royal, Bristol 1766-1966.*

Contents

Preface

Commissioned as part of the celebrations for the 50th anniversary of the Bristol Old Vic Theatre School, this book offers a glance back - from the perspective of 1996 - across half a century at one of the most prestigious theatre schools in the world.

Out of this School came many award-winning performers: Daniel Day-Lewis (1989 Best Actor Oscar for *My Left Foot*); Jeremy Irons (1990 Best Actor Oscar for *Reversal of Fortune*); Miranda Richardson (Golden Globe); Joanna Riding (Olivier Best Actress); Simon Cadell (Olivier Best Actor); and Jane Lapotaire (Emmy and others) to name but a few. Many others have been nominated for prestigious awards, recently including Pete Postlethwaite (Best Supporting Actor Oscar for the 1993 film *In The Name of the Father*) and Mark Lambert (Olivier Best Supporting Actor for his 1994 stage performance as Joxer in *Juno and the Paycock*).

Countless Bristol-trained performers are familiar faces on stage or screen, because the real achievement of the BOV Theatre School is not the few who reached the heights of fame, but the exceptionally large proportion of its graduates who found jobs within months of leaving, and then continued working for many years in an industry renowned for its high levels of unemployment.

From humble beginnings just after the Second World War with only two full time staff and a dozen or so full time students, the Bristol Old Vic Theatre School has trained well over two thousand workers in the crafts of acting, directing, designing, set building, prop making, wardrobe, stage management, lighting and sound. Leavers from every single year since 1947 are still actively involved in a 'profession' which has developed into a multi-million pound performance and presentation 'industry'. Even those whose lives took a different direction testify to the value of what they learned at the Theatre School: about themselves, about other people, about skills, about life.

The aim of this book has been not only to record the personalities and peculiarities of BOVTS, but also to provide an insight into the wide variety of backgrounds from which people come to a theatre school, the demanding and ingenious methods by which they learn their crafts, and the remarkable range of ways and places in which they later use them. Truly, all the world's a stage.

Shirley Brown
Bristol
May 1996

1. Ten reasons why the Bristol Old Vic Theatre School is special

ONE
It's an integral part of a professional producing theatre, the Bristol Old Vic Company:

Nearly half (44.5%) of all the students on its Acting courses between 1946 and 1996 have at some time appeared in professional productions with the BOV Company, many while still at the School. All students - both Acting and Technical - have practical experience in a real working environment through putting their own shows on the Bristol Old Vic's stages: the historic 18th century Theatre Royal; the modern New Vic Studio; and, between 1963 and 1979, Bristol's Little Theatre in nearby Colston Street.

TWO
Its teachers are versatile working professionals:

Every member of staff is still directly involved in the business. They are actors, directors, composers, musical directors, designers (of sets and costumes, sound and lighting), choreographers, fight arrangers, costumiers, stage managers, technicians, consultants. They don't just teach it, they do it.

'They've got a Principal who is also a working member of the profession. Chris Denys doesn't just talk theory about the theatre, he really knows it, he's trodden the boards himself for years,' says Jane Lapotaire.

'The staff here each have a specific focus, but we all have multi-disciplinary skills,' adds Musical Director Neil

Rhoden, who also trained in dance and design. 'Jonathan Howell's experience as a dancer, singer, actor and director makes him a better combat teacher, because he brings to stage fighting a sense of style, movement, and theatre which he perhaps wouldn't have if he hadn't got all those other skills as well. Gail Gordon is not only a dancer and choreographer, but also has a very keen sense of theatre. Chris Denys trained as an actor and a skater, and is also a playwright. Every time any of us do a show, we're bringing all those different elements to bear on the work.'

THREE
Its teaching is not tied to any single philosophy or method:

'There was no one "school of thought" and tutors would often contradict one another,' says Paul Panting. 'That's why the School turns out such individual and diverse performers. Everyone is forced to find their own path.'

'There wasn't a particular method that the training was being fitted into,' says John Caird. 'It was up to students at Bristol to make something of it for themselves. The fact that one had to exist so much on one's own wits was hard, but at the same time it meant that one learnt how to have a practical, personal attitude towards one's craft after one left the School.'

FOUR
It's run with the same kind of outlook, application, workload and discipline as a professional producing company, taking a realistic attitude to an industry which is also, occasionally, an art:

'We take the attitude that a student's first day here is the first day of their career and treat them as professionals in training,' says BOVTS Technical Stage Manager Brian Buttle.

'And in the process we forge friendships that go on being supportive for years after people leave.'

'The atmosphere was creative, but also very practical ... Chris Denys taught us to mould our dreams into practical realities,' writes Susan Tordoff.

'Chris Denys always emphasised to us what it was like in the real world,' says Victor McGuire. 'He instilled in me a workmanlike approach to the job. I remember him saying that acting can mean anything from being on stage at the RSC, to being Frosty the Snowman on a garage forecourt selling petrol. And most of us became jobbing actors. We don't have starry-eyed ideas about it - we work. Acting is about learning your lines, turning up on time and hitting your mark.'

FIVE
Its graduates get jobs:

'When people leave here,' says Chris Denys, 'they don't get a diploma, but they do get a job.'

'If you trained at Bristol Old Vic Theatre School, it's like saying you've been to Oxford or Cambridge - the top places - and you know you're very likely to be seen when you apply for jobs,' say the ex-students.

'If you're auditioning for a show, and you see someone has come from the Bristol Old Vic Theatre School,' says Julian Slade, 'you can be sure they'll be of a certain standard - you never get anybody from that school who's an absolute dud, never.'

SIX
And they go on working for a long time:

In 1996, leavers from every single year since 1947 are still involved in some directly relevant occupation. Over half of all those who ever took BOVTS Acting courses are still actively available for work as actors: 'There's something about Bristol actors. Every theatre company I work in there's always at least one other. They're very evenly spread throughout the business, right through from Hollywood to the jobbing actors in rep or telly or commercials.'

SEVEN
They achieve key positions in the industry, for example:

As Artistic Directors: *Currently (1996):* Neil Bartlett (Lyric Theatre, Hammersmith); Christopher Dunham (Palace Theatre, Westcliff); Deborah Paige (Sheffield, previously Salisbury); and Antony Tuckey (Wolsey Theatre, Ipswich). *Formerly:* George Roman (Billingham, Clwyd and Exeter); Jane Howell (Exeter Northcott); Alan Dossor (Liverpool Everyman); Robin Herford (Stephen Joseph Theatre in Scarborough); Kit Thacker (Torch Theatre, Milford Haven); Julian Oldfield (Chester Gateway); Joan Knight at Perth for 25 years until she retired (i.e. went freelance!) in 1993; and John David at the Bristol Old Vic between 1980 and 1986.

As directors, in theatre, film and television: Sean Aita, James Barlow, John Caird, Robert Carsen, Vanessa Dodd, Greg Doran, Karl James, Tim Luscombe, David Massarella, Jeremy Meadow, Veronica Needa, Gareth Tudor Price, Alistair Reid, James Runcie.

As agents: Michelle Braidman, Sheridan Fitzgerald, John Grantham, Rachel Kruger, Jeff McKenna, Stephanie Randall, Stella Richards.

As casting directors: Daphne Bates, Stephanie Booth, Siobhan Bracke, Anji Carroll, Gary Davy, Brian Wheeler.

In the BBC: Sam Breckman (Location Manager); Ruth Caleb (former Head of Drama, BBC Wales); Vivienne Cozens (TV Director); Cyril Gates (Head of Resources, BBC Manchester); Sally Hulke (formerly in charge of design at BBC Bristol); Humphrey Jaeger (Designer); Dawn Monaghan (Operations Executive, BBC Manchester); Carolyn Montagu (Producer); Marcia Wheeler (Drama Producer, Training Manager, and TV Representative on the National Council for Drama Training).

In independent production companies: Bill Butt (Atlas Adventures); Chris James (Watershed Television); Susannah Lipscombe (Cod Steaks); Trudie Styler (Xingu Films).

EIGHT
The BOV Theatre School has an excellent reputation all over the world. Graduates working abroad include:

Australia: John Bell (Artistic Director of The Bell Shakespeare, Sydney - 'Australia's National Shakespeare Company'); Ilona Rodgers (acted in several classic serials on BBC TV in the 1960s and 1970s, and was later described as 'the Dame Judi Dench of Australia and New Zealand'); David Henry Salter (Adelaide-based actor, director and teacher); Margaret Sadler Watson (one of the first intake at BOVTS in 1946, and in 1996 a director and festival adjudicator, and audio-describer for the Queensland State Theatre, helping sight-impaired people to enjoy performances).

Canada: Pat Armstrong, Rodger Barton, Bernard Behrens, Jocelyn Cunningham, Curzon Dobell, Lorne Kennedy, Tom Kneebone, Goldie Semple (actors); Robin Phillips (former Artistic Director of the Shakespeare Festival Theatre, Stratford, Ontario); Elliott Hayes (former literary manager in Stratford, Ontario, and a successful playwright in the early 1990s); Gabriel Prendergast (Professor of Theatre at the University of Regina in Saskatchewan).

Denmark: Henrik Larsen (actor); Vivienne McKee (Artistic Director of the English-speaking London Toast Theatre in Copenhagen).

Iceland: Gudmunder Finnsson (former Head of Sound at the National Theatre, then sound engineer/manager of ITR Audio Systems, part of Reykjavik's Sports and Youth Council); Heida Steindors (known as Ragnheidur Steindórsdóttir in Reykjavik, where she has acted with the National Theatre since 1984).

Malta: Ethel Farrugia (runs a Theatre School).

New Zealand: Brian Bell (well-known in television); Margaret Sadler Watson (director/adjudicator 1975-90).

Portugal: Gloria de Matos (at the National Theatre in Lisbon).
South Africa: Edwin Van Wyk (has a famous drag act 'along
the lines of Australia's Dame Edna Everage').
United States of America: John Allison (founded a New York
theatre company); Alan Fletcher (ran American Conservatory
Theatre - ACT - in San Francisco in the 1970s); Ian Frost
(Florida-based actor, who tours internationally with solo shows,
notably on Lord Byron); Christopher Selbie (Artistic Director of
Denver Civic Theatre, Colorado); Geoffrey Sherman (Artistic
Director of Meadow Brook Theatre, Michigan); John Tillinger
(Director at Long Wharf Theatre, New Haven and on
Broadway); Edward Evanko, Diana Van Fossen and Gene
Wilder (actors).

NINE
Yet the organisation is small and flexible enough to treat people as individuals - the School's higgledy-piggledy 'organically grown' premises provide a disciplined but informal creative environment:

'Being in a provincial city, people can live within
walking distance of the School and each other, which gives it a
strong sense of community.'
'It's a much closer environment than London where you
have to travel miles between places. Everything's right here,
arts-wise, and happening: it takes only a few minutes to get to
any of the cultural centres, Bristol Old Vic, the Colston Hall, the
Hippodrome, the Watershed Media Centre, the Arnolfini Gallery
and Cinema, the City Art Gallery and Museum.'
The Bristol Old Vic Theatre School is a very personal,
people-centred place. In the front garden are living memorials to
some of those who have passed through: most recently an oak
tree planted for ex-Principal Nat Brenner; in the middle a tulip
tree that was planted in the early 1970s by his wife Joan, to
replace an apple tree that died; a cherry tree for Daphne Heard,
who taught there in the 1950s and early 1960s; a laburnum for
student Madeleine Farrell, killed in a road accident in her second

term in 1988; and 'Bert's Bower', a flower-covered wooden archway commemorating Bert Male, who was the School's 'refreshingly down to earth' gardener for over twenty years until his death in 1995 aged 87. Every summer, the students have an end-of-year outdoor gathering which has become known as 'Bert's Garden Party', and the little room where he enjoyed his tea breaks has been festooned with photographs of him in his garden, and re-named 'Bert's Kitchen'.

'The School seems like a big house with a family living in it. It's old-fashioned, homely, comfortable, and everyone is very approachable - but you work so hard and you learn so much.'

TEN
Rather than encouraging students to aim for fame, The Bristol Old Vic Theatre School prepares people to work as members of a team in the ensemble tradition long associated with the glorious name of the Old Vic.

2. Old Vic - who he?

She, actually.

This 'Vic' is short for Victoria, the English Queen who was only a Princess and far from old in 1833 when her name was given to the newly-refurbished Royal Victoria (formerly Royal Coburg) Theatre in London's Waterloo Road, which was later the home of the famous Old Vic repertory company founded by Lilian Baylis and destined to become Britain's most popular and prestigious classical theatre.

Lilian Baylis was a remarkable theatre manager who established and ran popular London venues for drama, opera and ballet at the Old Vic and Sadler's Wells until her death in 1937. The work she began led directly to four of Britain's major cultural institutions: her Old Vic Company was the inspiration for the National Theatre; her Vic Wells Ballet became the Royal Ballet; her Sadler's Wells Opera Company became the English National Opera; and her summer season of theatre at Stratford-upon-Avon seeded what was to become the Royal Shakespeare Company.

Born in 1874, Lilian Baylis had given violin recitals as a child prodigy before accompanying her musician parents to South Africa, where she became one of the first music teachers in Johannesburg. Returning to England in 1895, she helped her aunt, Emma Cons, to run what was then officially called the Royal Victoria Temperance Music Hall and Coffee Tavern, but was already known affectionately as the 'Old Vic'. After her aunt's death in 1912, Miss Baylis took over as Director and set up a repertory company which specialised in productions of Shakespeare, performing all the plays in his First Folio between 1914 and 1923. Several members of this Old Vic Company were subsequently honoured for services to the theatre, among them Peggy Ashcroft, Edith Evans, John Gielgud, Alec Guinness, Laurence Olivier, Ralph Richardson and Sybil Thorndike. 'Old Vic' became a by-word for excellence in classical performance and production.

Under the auspices of the London Old Vic Company, Lilian Baylis set up the first Old Vic Dramatic School in 1933, with a conjuror on the staff to teach actors 'quick thinking'. John Moody was the Head of this School during its wartime evacuation to the Cotswolds. In April 1946, French actor and director Michel Saint-Denis, who had trained young actors at his own London Theatre Studio between 1936 and 1939, founded a new London Old Vic Theatre School which began at the bomb-damaged theatre in the Waterloo Road, and moved in 1949 to new premises in East Dulwich. Its students included Val May (Artistic Director of the Bristol Old Vic Company from 1961 to 1975) and three future members of the BOVTS staff: Michael Ackland (Head of Technical Courses from 1955 to 1961); Richard Ainley (Principal from 1961 to 1963); and Adrian Cairns (Associate Principal from 1964 until 1989).

Michel Saint-Denis was one of three directors of a complementary Young Vic Company which was set up to offer work to an ensemble of promising young actors in touring plays for young people. All three taught at the London Old Vic Theatre School, and made a distinctive mark in the professional theatre: Saint-Denis' enthusiasm for ensemble playing has profoundly influenced the training of actors for generations; George Devine later founded the ground-breaking English Stage Company at the Royal Court; and Glen Byam Shaw directed the Stratford Memorial Theatre (forerunner of the RSC) for four years. The London Old Vic Theatre School opened in January 1947, but because of internal disagreements within the parent Company it was closed in 1952.

The Bristol Old Vic Company also began as one of the Old Vic's optimistic post-war enterprises, a regional offshoot which remained an integral part of the London Company until 1963. Ever since it was founded in 1946, the BOV Company has been based at the city's Theatre Royal, in King Street. Originally built in 1766, this horseshoe-shaped auditorium is Britain's oldest theatre building with a history of continuous use as a playhouse. Over the centuries it has been adapted and re-shaped to suit its changing times, most recently in 1970-72, when a versatile modern studio was added.

During the war, when the surrounding dockside area was Bristol's equivalent of London's old Covent Garden market, the

Theatre was very nearly turned into a greengrocery warehouse. After the severe bombing of the Bristol Blitz in May 1941, the 'Old Gaff' (as the Theatre Royal was then known) had been forced to close, and was sold at auction on 28 January 1942. Through the efforts of a small but energetic group who raised both the profile and the funds, the greengrocer was outbid by a Trust representing the theatre-loving citizens of Bristol, and in the autumn of 1942, C.E.M.A. (the wartime Council for the Encouragement of Music and the Arts, and forerunner of the Arts Council) assumed responsibility for the restoration and maintenance of the building.

The Bristol Theatre Royal re-opened with a visiting production of *She Stoops To Conquer* by the London Old Vic Company on 11 May 1943, when Sybil Thorndike, dressed as Mrs Hardcastle, delivered a specially-written Prologue by Herbert Farjeon. Two of Miss Thorndike's grandchildren, Benedict and Teresa Campbell, later trained as actors at the BOV Theatre School.

On 11 December 1945, just four months after VJ Day marked the official end of the war, the London Old Vic publicly announced its plan to create the resident Company in Bristol and appointed Hugh Hunt as the first Director. The Bristol Old Vic launched its opening season on 19 February 1946 with a production of Farquhar's *The Beaux' Stratagem*.

Hugh Hunt put the idea of a complementary theatre school to both the governors and the Arts Council in the early summer of 1946. Neither was enthusiastic. Even after the governors had been persuaded, the Arts Council still vetoed the proposed scheme. At that time they were still heavily committed to Michel Saint-Denis' London Old Vic Theatre School, and wary of potential problems. Nevertheless the Arts Council did eventually agree to the establishment of a BOV Theatre School, and even offered a modest annual guarantee against loss of £250, provided that the School would aim to be self-supporting, and that financial responsibility would rest entirely with the Old Vic.

In June the BOV Company officially announced its intention to establish the Theatre School as part of an 'Old Vic Theatre Plan', which would include offering those who showed the necessary talent a chance to start their professional career with the Old Vic, either in Bristol or in London. But it was another four months before the School was officially opened, on 21 October 1946.

As a leading actor with the London Old Vic, Laurence Olivier made a speech at the Theatre Royal to mark the occasion, but did not actually venture across the road to the School itself. Although Edward Stanley, the School's first Director, had an office in the Theatre Royal, the School's own premises were the upstairs room of number 27 Queen Charlotte Street, where the downstairs was occupied by Powell Harvey and Co. Ltd., wholesale fruit merchants.

'That was where now Telecom is - opposite the stage door of the Theatre Royal,' recalls Rudi Shelly, a member of the staff since 1946. 'There was a little brick building, two floors, and the whole house reeked all the time of rotting onions and oranges. So if our School would get a coat of arms one of these days it should have a rotten onion in it - just to remind ourselves where we originally came from!'

3. 1946-54 Across the street and above the vegetables

Principal: Edward Stanley

In the years after the Second World War, the cobbled streets around Bristol's Theatre Royal were bustling with wheelbarrows going to and from the market across the road in Baldwin Street, and with barrels of ale being rolled from the holds of ships docked alongside the Llandoger Trow: 'The wonderful stench of rotting fruit and vegetables mixed with beer from the pubs, flowers from the flower markets and the very, very exciting smells of actresses, make-up, size and paint from the old Theatre Royal were very special.'

The frontage of the old Theatre Royal was two old houses with a small canopy and a narrow corridor leading into the small foyer. The stage door was at the end of a lane called The Rackhay, directly opposite the building that originally housed the Theatre School. The gap between 27 Queen Charlotte Street and its nearest neighbour, the Old Duke pub, was one of many scars left on Bristol by the bombing. Times were hard and almost everything was in short supply and on ration - food, clothes, materials for building, fuel for heating. But the war was over, and there was a marvellous feeling of optimism, of starting again, and that anyone could do anything. Undaunted and resourceful, the Bristol Old Vic actors wore their overcoats during rehearsals, and the set-builders did ingenious things with bits of aeroplanes and debris. For the School's 1948 end-of-year production of *The Yellow Jacket,* the temple roof was made from parts of the fuselage of a surplus Horsa glider!

It's unclear how Edward Stanley came to be chosen as the first Director of the BOV Theatre School. He grew up in London's East End and won a scholarship to go to university but went into banking because his family could not afford to support him. During military service in the 1940s in Cairo, he was both a director and an actor with the New Vic Players, helping to boost the morale of the troops in the Middle East. When he applied for the Bristol post, he was working as a director at Perth Rep, from where he brought to Bristol as his Assistant Director a young actress, Joan Cairncross. When the School first opened, they were the only two members of staff.

Edward Stanley has been described - with affection, not implied criticism - as 'a passionate amateur'. Where many theatre professionals affect a world-weary cynicism about their work, he never lost the enthusiasm of someone who was involved with it for pleasure rather than money, describing the theatre in a 1952 speech to Weston-super-Mare's Dramatic Society as 'a most exciting thing'.

He is remembered as a handsome and magnetically charming man with a resonant voice and a natural skill as a teacher, though some of his students were disconcerted to hear him claim, with no hint of regret, that he had never had a day's training in his life. 'He would give you all his attention, drawing on his cigarette while he was considering what you were doing,' recalls Susan Dowdall. 'You could feel his brain buzzing away, and he made very telling comments.'

Joan Cairncross, who had trained at Guildhall, was not much older than the Bristol students and, she says, 'certainly younger than a lot of the evening ones!' While the full time classes were intended for would-be professionals, BOVTS also offered evening classes for enthusiastic amateurs, who were an important source of income for the School in its early years.

Miss Cairncross - no relation to BOV Company actor James Cairncross - remembers her time at the Theatre School as very busy: 'We had all the normal day students and then evening classes two nights a week for two groups. And we were also doing bits of adjudicating around Bristol while we were trying to pull the whole thing together. Edward left most of the voice training to me, and a certain amount of music, and we both did mime and improvisation and those sort of things.' It was exhausting: within a year, she decided to go back to being an actress.

After two weeks, serendipity brought to the School a third member of staff who was to stay with BOVTS through all the vicissitudes of the first fifty years and to become a legend in the training of actors not only in Bristol but all over the world:

'I arrived,' says 88-year-old Rudi Shelly, in his distinctive mid-European accent, 'in November 1946, and I've been here ever since, a sort of superannuated doormat.'

Born in Austria on 9 May 1908, Raphael Shelly began acting while a student in Germany (he has a PhD in Economics) and worked as a professional dancer before Hitler's rise to power prompted him to emigrate. In 1936 he arrived in Palestine, where he had a day job as an Inspector for the British Mandate Government, and was also a member of the Education and Entertainment Corps. Language difficulties did not prevent him from getting involved in play-reading groups, giving illustrated lectures to British soldiers, and directing amateur Army shows. Through these voluntary activities he acquired letters of recommendation which led to being invited to England as the first foreign student ever accepted to study stage direction. Happily for Bristol, he was assigned to the Old Vic, where Director Hugh Hunt seized his opportunity to provide the fledgling Theatre School with a movement teacher.

More teachers were gradually recruited to the staff. Isabel Chisman, who taught mime there in the 1940s, was something of a pioneer: the first West Country woman to appear on television; and the author of a book on *Mime as Used to Meet Social Needs,* the first of its kind. She had also been Arts Adviser to the National Union of Townswomen's Guilds, and was perhaps an oddly inappropriate teacher for the young men who had recently left military service, several of whom remember only that she lived in Bath and wore a wig.

'A wonderful character,' recalls Norman Rossington. 'About nine feet tall, with pince nez, and she used to say "Quiet dears"!'; 'She was very sweet, and a fairly big lady, who wore these awful black tights,' laughs William Eedle, who used to have to partner her and lift her for demonstrations; 'My abiding memory of this lady, whom we used to rather irreverently call "Issy Chissy" is when she adjudicated an amateur festival at the Theatre Royal,' says Ken Woodward. 'On the last night the curtain went down and when it rose again she was sitting in a beautiful gold chair in a magnificent gown, looking absolutely superb.'

Edith Manvell, who was for a time the School's Assistant Director, was the wife of BBC film critic Roger

Manvell, and taught voice, speech, mime and theatre history at BOVTS from 1948 until 1957: 'I don't know if she did actually wear chiffon scarves, but she was that sort of person,' says Mary Steele, who played Queen Elizabeth I in a spectacular public pageant for the 1953 coronation, with fellow students as her courtiers on a gilded barge which sailed up the River Avon to Bristol city centre. Others recall Mrs Manvell as very clever, but somewhat aloof, and sometimes sharp-tongued: Roy Skelton remembers a voice class when she told him he'd make a good mime artist! Ironically, he has made a long and successful career out of voice work, notably as the original voice of *Dr Who's* Daleks, and for twenty years the voice of his own creations Zippy and George in TV's *Rainbow*. Bob Harris, who always enjoyed the funny side of life, particularly remembers Mrs Manvell as the Mother Superior in the BOV's 1952 production of *Measure for Measure:* 'When Isabella complained about not having enough privileges, Edith would put her arms below her breasts, rather like a pantomime Dame, lift them up and say "Are not these large enough?"!'

Actor Anthony Holland joined the staff as Edward Stanley's Assistant Director in 1950 and stayed until 1957, teaching acting, stage fighting and later stage management, while running seaside summer seasons in the holidays. His particular interest was in fencing, and he was Honorary Secretary of the Gloucestershire Amateur Fencing Union, which was based at the Bristol Theatre Royal.

Number 27 Queen Charlotte Street was quite a handsome, slightly decorated, redbrick building, probably built around 1880. Everyone would gather there in the mornings, coming through the front door past a closed door to the left (behind which were the cabbages and cauliflowers) and up the stairs to the top floor where there was one big room with a wooden floor, sloping ceiling, one small lavatory, a large fireplace, a piano, and lockers where students kept such essentials as a *Complete Shakespeare,* an *Oxford Book of English Verse,* a fencing foil, tights and jockstrap. The room was occasionally transformed into a theatre, with an invited audience for productions, including Hsiung's *Lady Precious Stream* in 1947, and Rattigan's *French Without Tears* in 1952. If there were not enough chairs to go round, people would sit on handy orange boxes instead. The School's very first production was a Thornton Wilder one-acter called *The Long Christmas Dinner,* 'and it was very, very long,' sighs Gwenllian Davies.

At first, all the classes were held in that one room at 'the fruit school', as it was sometimes called. Later, students were able to do voice production practice on the stage of the Theatre Royal, and classes were also held in the Theatre bars and in the hall and courtyards of Saint Nicholas Church School, which used to stand to the left of the stage door, where there is now a tower block called Rackhay House. The yards had 'sloping tarmac and drains that you could fall into when you danced the can-can, which I did,' chuckles Rita McKerrow, who was one of the first evening students in 1946, and has taught singing at BOVTS since 1975. Quite a number of former students later joined the School staff: among the first was Jack Moss, an affable military sort of chap with a raffish moustache, who did evening classes in the early years, later became the Bursar and taught PE, and appeared in productions with both the School and the Company.

Despite its early limitations of space and scope, the BOV Theatre School did have the great advantage of being an integral part of a highly respected working repertory company, for which its students were a source of cheap and willing labour. While the School was based in Queen Charlotte Street, the students were in daily contact with the professional actors and technicians at the Theatre Royal, who were presenting a varied programme of classics and new plays, usually with three weeks' rehearsal and three week runs. Students were invited to watch Company dress rehearsals in the Theatre Royal (a tradition that continued until the mid-1980s) and they would often work backstage and appear in the professional productions, filling the crowd scenes or playing small parts, getting experience of both the excitement and the discipline of theatre.

The students and the Company also mingled socially, eating in such memorable establishments as Mrs Balch's café next to the Theatre in King Street - popularly known as 'Hell's Kitchen' - where the atmosphere was lively and bohemian, and the menu featured pies, eggs, chips, giant doorsteps of bread and butter and hot mugs of tea, at very affordable prices. Many recall Mrs B as a sort of unofficial Arts Council, subsidising the actors and students with beans on toast on tick. For a treat, they would go to Marco's Italian restaurant up the steps in Baldwin Street, where Marco Berni would allow theatre students to order only soup and sweet, or a plate of plain spaghetti, in extraordinarily generous portions.

On their way to and from the Theatre and the School, students also encountered the contrasting characters of the greengrocery trade, immortalised in an end-of-first-term revue song in 1953 (to the tune of *Down in Covent Garden* by Alan Melville):

Men: Two Welsh Back market porters.

Girls: Two Old Vic supporters.

All: Two vastly different couples whom you'd think were poles apart.

Men: We're hale and rather hearty.

Girls: We're pale and rather arty.

Men: Our lives we pledge to fruit and veg,

Girls: Ours we devote to Art.

Men: At 4am you'll find us up and doing,
           Loading up the lorries in the dawn's first light.

Girls: At 4am you'll find us grimly queuing,
           For Yvonne's playing 'Cleo' there tonight!

Men: Cabbages and cauliflowers,

Girls: Carey and Coulette,

Men: Working ruddy awful hours,

Girls: Queuing in the wet.

Men: Ripe tomatoes, lovely leeks,
           We prefer George Robey.

Girls: Queuing up for weeks and weeks,
           To yell at Alan Dobie.

In 1947, Bristol was the first British university to establish a Department of Drama, which remained the only one until 1961, when Hugh Hunt was appointed the first Professor of Drama at Manchester. While Mr Hunt was Director of the BOV Company in the 1940s, Bristol offered what was then a unique combination of academic and vocational training: among the lecturers who taught at both University and Theatre School were Glynne Wickham (who in 1960 became the first Professor of Drama in Bristol - and in Britain), Classics Professor H D F Kitto, and theatre architect Richard Southern. For many years

Bristol boasted a famous 'triangle' of Theatre School, Repertory Company and University Drama Department, promising a three-sided perspective of vocational training, professional production and theoretical study, but in practice the relationship was always strongest between School and Company.

The University Drama Department's most practical contribution to the Theatre School was the opportunity to work in its studio theatre on the first floor of the gothic-style Wills Building at the top of Park Street. This studio, which was the first flexible theatre of its kind in Britain, was converted from its original use as a sports hall by Richard Southern, and was the main performance space for both University and Theatre School between 1951 and 1967. 'The stage was built with rostra, which we moved about to show how versatile it was,' says Phyllida Law, who was one of those who took part in the opening performance at the Drama Studio.

'It was a totally open square space, and you could set it up to suit whatever style of theatre you wanted to do,' recalled Roger Jeffery, who was BOVTS Technical Director in the 1960s. 'It had a flying grid, and a little balcony, which was the original balcony for viewing the squash. And it could seat about a hundred, on stacking chairs that could be put anywhere.'

'It was an interesting and highly flexible stage,' adds University lecturer George Brandt, 'but suffered from the enormous drawback of being just across the passage from the great organ in the Great Hall, which meant that not only whenever there was an event on, but whenever the organist was practising, we couldn't hear ourselves think!'

Half a mile away, in Clifton, was another School which was closely linked with the Theatre School for many years: the Bristol School of Dancing, which was owned and run by Mary Hoskyn and Muriel Carpenter in the 1950s, and by Lynn Britt from 1964 through the 1970s. Its premises, at 55 and 57 Pembroke Road (neighbouring the modern Catholic cathedral) are now converted back to their original use as two private houses, but formerly provided lodgings as well as practice rooms for students.

Julian Slade recalls that Muriel and Mary used to come to Queen Charlotte Street once a week to take classes, and sometimes the students went up to Clifton: 'I wasn't awfully good at dancing but the lessons were hilarious and the ladies were marvellous.' Later, when Julian was working for the Company, he would stay with them, as did many other Theatre School people including Phyllida Law, Annette Crosbie and Bernard Behrens. Peter Baldwin, who describes Mary as 'the sensible one who ran the place and did most of the cooking' and Muriel as 'the eccentric ballet mistress', burnt many a midnight candle around the wonderful Aga stove in their kitchen. Those who know him only as *Coronation Street*'s Derek Wilton may be surprised to learn that Peter was a promising and enthusiastic ballet dancer while at BOVTS in the mid-1950s: 'I did two big programmes with the School of Dancing in the Theatre Royal: one was *Coppelia;* the other was a group of ballets, including one choreographed specially for me by Liz West.'

Elizabeth West, who lived at the ballet school, was part of a trio of student friends with Julian Slade and Phyllida Law. She was the original choreographer of Julian's Bristol Old Vic Company musicals *Salad Days, The Merry Gentleman* and *Christmas in King Street,* and co-founder (with Peter Darrell) of the Western Theatre Ballet Company, which eventually became the Scottish Theatre Ballet. Her career was tragically cut short when she was killed in a freak accident on an Austrian mountain in the early 1960s: 'The School of Dancing was haunted by her after that,' reveals BOVTS Movement teacher Aubrey Budd, whose sister had been trained by Miss West. 'Up in one of the studios, a crack appeared in the window in the shape of "E W". You could be downstairs in the kitchen and hear her swishing about, doing class upstairs. She used to come back because she loved it so much.'

Students describe the Theatre School in the early days as being 'very Stanislavski orientated', though Edward Stanley himself insisted, when interviewed by *Theatre World* in 1947, that it subscribed to no particular dogmatic teaching of convention, movement, acting, or thought and simply aimed to help each student to become 'a sensitive instrument sensitised by every means we know of or can develop, balanced and controlled by a live and exploring mind, seeking always true harmony of thought, feeling and technical expression.'

Recognising that his students were 'likely to find themselves in weekly repertory, non-stop West End runs, and

working in the best, and the worst, of the British theatre', Mr
Stanley maintained that 'provided they are instilled with the
highest standards, a sound and readily available technique will
enable them to withstand onslaughts upon their values.'

Edward Stanley kept the School going in 'a wonderful
happy muddle' for eight years despite great difficulties: the
premises and facilities were inadequate; the staff were
underpaid and, in some cases, inexperienced or inefficient; and
Denis Carey, who took over from Hugh Hunt as Director of the
BOV Company in 1950, had 'frankly never taken a very great
interest in it' according to Charles Landstone in his book about
The Bristol Old Vic, the first ten years. There were other worries
too, including a damaging rift between Mr Stanley and his
Assistant Director Anthony Holland.

These pressures transformed an outgoing and talented
man into a troubled and frustrated one. During a heated
discussion about some aspect of School policy, Edward Stanley
declared his intention to resign, and left in May 1954. He
remained based in Bristol, where he taught in several local
schools, while also working part time as a lecturer at Hull
University. He continued his involvement in amateur drama -
notably with Bath's Octagon Theatre Club - adjudicating
performances, and teaching at his own studio in Bath's Abbey
Churchyard. From 1961 until his death in 1972, aged 58, he
taught drama at Hendon College in Middlesex.

Edward Stanley later regretted his hasty resignation,
which came, ironically, just before the opening, on 1 June 1954,
of *Salad Days,* the musical show which was to help take the
School out of the vegetable warehouse and into its next phase of
development.

4. 1954-61 Downside Road and sunny side up

Principal: Duncan Ross

Soon after Edward Stanley's departure as Director of BOVTS, John Moody was appointed by the Bristol Old Vic as Director of both the Company and the Theatre School. He had been involved with the avant-garde Group Theatre in the 1930s, and an actor at the London Old Vic, which was where he met Duncan Ross. Though never a student at the London Old Vic Theatre School, Ross had also been an actor with the London Old Vic Company, as well as leader of Michel Saint-Denis' Young Vic Company for three years of touring. At John Moody's invitation, he moved to Bristol from Nottingham (where he had been Manager of the Playhouse Theatre) in the late summer of 1954, and was Principal of the Theatre School until the winter of 1961.

Though known officially by his middle name, Duncan was always 'Bill' to those who knew him personally. Bristol colleagues pay tribute to him as 'a vital and energetic teacher', 'wise and gifted', and 'a unique phenomenon as a teacher in the theatre'. Students remember his dynamic persona, his forthright views - and his hair, variously described as 'unruly red-blond' or 'glowing ginger'.

Until 1954, any hopes of the Theatre School expanding into larger premises had always been thwarted by the Bristol Old Vic's lack of funds. But the Company had an unexpected windfall which made it possible for the School to move to its present buildings overlooking Clifton Downs, a vast green open space where generations of students have taken invigorating runs first thing in the morning, practised fighting with a variety of weapons, and made films on location.

'We grew out of that post-war hardship,' recalled Nat Brenner, who was Production Manager for the BOV Company in the early 1950s. 'The School needed decent premises, and fortunately *Salad Days* came along as a spring musical in 1954 - the title came from Shakespeare's *Antony and Cleopatra,* which we'd recently done, the quotation was from Cleopatra, who talks about "my salad days, when I was young and green". The press were extremely favourable - except for two, Ken Tynan, who loathed it, and Milton Shulman of the *Evening Standard* - but everyone else was very happy about it, and so were the public. It ran, and made some money. And a little bit of it came to the School.'

Julian Slade and Dorothy Reynolds had written *Salad Days* as a jolly local show incorporating lots of little topical jokes about the plays that had been performed in that BOV season and the actors who were in them. No-one had any idea that it would go to London and be a huge popular success at a time when American extravaganzas like *South Pacific* and *Guys and Dolls* were all the rage.

'But the road had been paved by *The Boyfriend,* which had opened about two months before and had proved that a small British show could be a thundering success,' says Julian Slade, who had begun his career as a composer and musical director with the BOV Company in 1952 after a year as a student actor at the Theatre School. He left Bristol with *Salad Days* in August 1954, and stayed with the show at London's Vaudeville Theatre for its first two years.

Salad Days has proved enduringly popular, and the BOV Theatre School has paid an ongoing tribute to it with anniversary productions in 1984, 1989 and 1994. Pippa Haywood still vividly recalls playing Lady Raeburn in 1984: 'Hearing six hundred people roar with laughter was a quite ecstatic feeling - as if you'd just given them all a wonderful present!'

The show's wonderful present to the Theatre School amounted to £7,000, which, together with a grant from the Dulverton Trust, provided sufficient funds for the two Victorian villas on the corner of Downside Road to be purchased - for £6,000 - and then converted, which cost another £12,000.

The Downside Road buildings were officially opened on 26 June 1956, with speeches by Dame Sybil Thorndike and Sir Lewis Casson, but by then the School had already been working there for several months. There were many fewer students and classes in those days, and a large part of one of the houses was given over to the Principal and his family as living accommodation. When the Ross family moved into 2 Downside Road in the autumn of 1955, they had a drawing room, a children's play room, one bedroom, a bathroom and a kitchen on the first floor, and two more bedrooms on the top floor. But the whole of number 1 was converted into studios and classrooms, as was the ground floor of number 2, where the Principal had a small office.

'I suppose I did rather feel like a house mother,' recalls Marianne Ross, who had two small children at that time. 'We were in the School a lot, and the students used to come into our apartment. Bill would sometimes direct plays at the Theatre Royal and the actors from the Bristol Old Vic used to come for tea and homemade bread and cakes.'

Julian Slade recalls that he and Denis Carey and Dorothy Reynolds each had a letter asking if they would allow a room at Downside Road to be named after them. 'Denis wrote back to say yes he'd be delighted; I wrote back and said I'd be delighted and hoped there would be a piano in "my" room; Dorothy Reynolds wrote to say "Yes, if you lock the door and send me the key" - she was never at a drama school herself and she didn't approve of them!'

While the School was based in Queen Charlotte Street, it was easy to use the BOV Company's workshops to make props, sets and costumes, and Technical students had been treated very much as apprentices, spending most of their time working alongside the professionals in the Theatre. With the move to Downside Road came the setting up of the School's own Technical workshops, and the appointment of Michael Ackland as 'Head of Design', which, he says 'turned out to be something of an understatement' as he was given responsibility for setting up the whole Technical course in the new premises, and teaching not only design and theatre history but also electrics and stage management. In this he was greatly helped by John Lavender who, as Technical Director for the University Drama Department, ran the Drama Studio and 'not only filled in the gaps in my knowledge but also made everything happen'.

The Theatre School shared with the University not only the Drama Studio but also an interest in new writing for the stage. Duncan Ross's students undertook the production of original scripts written by postgraduate students in the Drama Department - and most famously of the first play by Harold Pinter, *The Room:* 'Henry Woolf, who was a student at Bristol University and a great friend of mine, produced the play at the Drama Department in May 1957,' writes Mr Pinter. 'In January 1958, Duncan Ross directed the play with the Bristol Old Vic Theatre School. This production was seen by Harold Hobson of the *Sunday Times* and reviewed enthusiastically. This review led Michael Codron, the London Theatre producer, to produce my first full length play, *The Birthday Party,* in 1958.' From the mid-1950s, the Drama Department offered a bursary for theatre practitioners, among them playwright John Arden, whose play *The Happy Haven* was premiered in the Drama Studio as a combined University-Theatre School production and later seen at the Royal Court.

The second half of the 1950s was an exhilarating time, when the first generation of 'teenagers' were gathering in new-fangled 'coffee bars' and discovering radical new ideas in music, theatre and entertainment. American film director Elia Kazan put moody Marlon Brando *On The Waterfront* and sent rebellious James Dean *East of Eden.* Bill Haley rocked around the clock, Elvis Presley got *All Shook Up,* skiffle star Lonnie Donegan was *Puttin' on the Style* - and at London's Royal Court Theatre, Director George Devine presented the play that seemed to speak for all the young disaffected jazz-loving, artistic working class boys whose lives had been transformed by education - John Osborne's *Look Back in Anger.*

Britain was going through an exciting phase, and Bristol was a city of some significance: 'There was nowhere else like it in the country when I went there in 1958,' says Stephanie Cole. 'It was the only city outside London with a first-rate drama school and a number one rep theatre. And the only university in the country with a drama department. Plus it had the Colston Hall, the Hippodrome and the Little Theatre. It was a unique situation where everything could feed into everything else.'

While Duncan Ross was Principal of the Theatre School, the BOV Company had three different Directors: John Hale - 'a very jolly ex-Navy man, who was a great encourager of students' - replaced John Moody in 1959, and was himself superseded by Val May in 1961. Some unfortunate romantic entanglements between members of the Company and students at the School led Duncan Ross to try and protect his students from what he viewed as 'moral danger', so they were officially forbidden to socialise with the actors, though the rule proved impossible to enforce. Later, Duncan Ross came to believe that the students were being used by the Bristol Old Vic as cheap labour, and not really being helped to develop their talents, which caused a little schism between himself and then General Manager Nat Brenner, who insisted the experience was good for the students as well as economical for the Company.

Ross's innovative and holistic approach to the training of actors made him a profound and inspirational influence on his staff as well as his students. His ideas were developed from his work with Michel Saint-Denis, his study of Stanislavski - whom he admired but did not entirely agree with, saying 'an actor prepares, but then an actor *acts* - you could go on preparing for ever' - and of the methods used by the Actors' Studio in New York: 'He aimed to marry the physical techniques of mental, physical and vocal dexterity with a root understanding of a character's emotional reality,' explains Chris Tranchell.

Ruth Caleb sees Ross as 'a figure of the sixties - experimenting with new styles of teaching, and encouraging new styles of acting to accommodate the new wave of writers who were emerging', and sums up his regime as 'physical exercise and a direct assault on our emotions and our imagination, coupled with giving us the basic tools of the trade'. He was very keen on all-round physical development, and introduced judo, gymnastics and horseriding lessons as an integral part of the training.

Ross's basic intention was to encourage invention and imagination so as to develop initiative, freedom and a sense of responsibility in the individual, alongside a willingness to merge personal qualities into the ensemble, creating what Michel Saint-Denis had called 'the unity of general effect': 'Everybody was part of a team,' explains Stephanie Cole. 'You were part of a company and the play was the important thing. I think that made you a better actor because the whole was more important than your individual contribution.'

Duncan Ross's small and loyal staff of only five full

time teachers worked closely together, with a sense of striving for a common aim rather than specialising in any particular area of skill. Rudi Shelly, Daphne Heard, Maggie Collins, John Oxley and Michael Ackland each constantly reinforced and supplemented what the others were doing. Several of the staff also taught on annual summer courses at Dartington Hall in Devon and Dillington House in Somerset.

As an actress Daphne Heard, who taught Voice and Acting classes at the School between 1955 and 1962, played major stage roles in rep (including Bristol Old Vic) and the West End, and memorably portrayed Peter Bowles' mother in television's *To The Manor Born*. Peggy Ann Wood describes her as 'very much the old-fashioned leading lady' and students were impressed by her stylish physical presence and 'ramrod straight' back: 'Daphne was left over from the days when girls were taught how to walk,' says Milton Johns. 'She didn't walk across a room, she floated. Her carriage was superb.' Fellow-teacher Maggie Collins remembers Daphne as 'a "Britannia's sister" sort of lady', whose capacious handbag seemed ever full of every possible practical requirement. Many remember her advice, in the days before credit cards, to hang on to some valuable item that could be pawned to provide emergency funds: 'She had a solid silver teapot which had been "popped" on more than one occasion to pay the train fare to a new engagement,' writes Clive Rust. With characteristic generosity, Daphne once told a group of young students who had just moved into a shared flat that she had something for them, and produced a Baby Belling cooker - not, in that case, from the handbag.

Australian Maggie Collins, who trained as an actress at RADA, taught Acting classes at BOVTS between spring 1959 and July 1962, and is remembered for 'her unremitting vivaciousness and cheerful manner'. She had worked as an actress in various British reps, and also in Australia with the Elizabethan Theatre Trust Touring company, directed by Hugh Hunt.

'We did work very closely together at the Theatre School,' says Maggie, who later taught at LAMDA. 'Bill Ross used to monitor our classes perhaps once a week, and there was a lovely atmosphere of co-operation. He used to say he was on "a kind of search for a procedure" - he wouldn't use the word "method" - in which everything evolved from the given conditions for each piece of work. Every project was a personal exploration for him and for everyone involved, and never solidified into rigid theory.'

Nevertheless, Ross did have his own ideas and system, which he formulated during his time at BOVTS into a text book intended for use only within the School, where it became known - not altogether respectfully - as 'The Bible'. This book joined a reading list for young actors that included not only the classic Stanislavski books, *An Actor Prepares* and *Building A Character,* but also a philosophically challenging book called *Zen in the Art of Archery,* encouraging the students to think about such ideas as that the arrow shoots itself - and apply it to their craft by developing a natural and relaxed manner on stage. In other words - as Rudi Shelly has put it to generations of earnestly trying young actors - 'Don't work so hard!'

Stanislavski's insistence that the actor should wholeheartedly believe in himself as the character he's playing had an unexpected practical spin-off for George Roman: 'One of my fellow-students, Leader Hawkins, was the proud owner of a Ford Prefect, in which he undertook the daunting task of teaching me to drive. On the day of my test he said, exasperated, trying to boost my confidence: "As a good student of the Stanislavski Method, try to *believe* for the duration of the test that you *can* drive." And I passed!'

'And once you've learned to drive,' adds Maggie Collins, 'Bill Ross would have said, "Let the car drive itself" - just like the Zen arrow.'

For non-actors, the course was only one year, but as Michael Ackland remembers: 'The whole tone and philosophy of the School originated from Duncan Ross and his ideas of style and acting "truth". This was its strength. The humblest non-Acting student who only wanted to learn about lighting could not go through the course without gaining an insight into Ross's ideas and theory of theatre, and would be expected to study the play with almost the same intensity as the actors.'

The great value of Ross's theories, Mr Ackland explains, 'was that they made all participants in the production think about what they were doing. He tried to fit all aspects of a theatrical event into a pattern, eliminating as far as possible the kind of arbitrary whim which could easily lead to an unsatisfactory blend of styles in acting, scenery, props or whatever. His central focus was a progression between "reality" at one end of the scale and "formality" at the other, with many transitional states in between. Take as example a chair: starting at the realistic end with a real chair; moving along to a real chair with the highlights on the limbs picked out, the upholstery painted or, say, the whole chair painted white; then along a bit further, where the chair becomes fifty per cent larger than it should be; then further, where it is formalised into just four legs, or a back and legs, then perhaps a square cube; and finally no chair at all as the actors do not sit down. Or think of Dali's surrealistic painting of melting clocks: realistic objects presented in a form and environment that are formalised in varying degrees. Within any single production, various elements might be at different points in the scale, but they would be where they were for a reason.'

For a man in the vanguard of new approaches to training actors, Ross was surprisingly Victorian in some of his attitudes, and very strict not only about punctuality and morals, but even about dress codes: the boys were expected to wear grey flannel trousers, white shirt, tie and a smart casual jacket; and the girls a 'modest' style of dress or skirt. Women who worked as stage managers in the early 1960s recall that they were not allowed to wear trousers, and that rule extended to female student actors as well as 'techies' (technicians).

All students signed a strict contract agreeing to obey the School rules and work hard on penalty of being asked to leave. Saturday morning classes were compulsory, but Milton Johns recalls that attendance used to drop off halfway through the term - 'and then the riot act would be read. It was a very disciplined atmosphere - and none the worse for that. There was also a very disciplined atmosphere when you started to work as an ASM in the Company. We arrived the day before everyone else and were given a good lecture on how we should conduct ourselves: when on theatre business, for example, we were never to address a member of the Company as other than Mr or Miss.'

Marianne Ross recalls an amusing illustration of how deeply ingrained this outward show of respect was, even in disrespectful circumstances: a student who feared he would be asked to leave the School made plans to get his own back by planting bulbs in the garden which would come up in the spring spelling 'Up you, Mr Ross'!

In 1960, Duncan Ross presented the BOV Trust's School Management Committee with a five-year plan for extending the resources of the School, perhaps building a small studio at the back, and offering the staff longer contracts and cost-of-living increases as a reward for loyalty and an incentive to stay. The Trust refused to make the necessary financial commitment, which left the School's staff feeling frustrated and under-valued. After six intensely creative years fired by Duncan Ross's charismatic enthusiasm, Michael Ackland was exhausted by the relentless hard work and lack of resources, and no longer able to summon up the recurring enthusiasm to start each autumn term saying 'This is a screwdriver' to a new group of would-be backstage workers. He left in the summer of 1961, and followed two different careers using the same sort of attention to detail that is required in theatre design and technical work: as a jeweller; and as an entomologist working on fly taxonomy for Oxford University Museum, where he worked full time for ten years and became an Honorary Associate Curator in 1992.

Duncan Ross resigned as Principal of the BOV Theatre School in May 1961, and left in December for America, where his Bristol work with visiting Fullbright scholars had earned him such high esteem that he had had offers from seven universities to run their drama departments. He went first to Seattle, then to Montreal, where he ran the Canadian National Theatre School for two years, returning to Seattle in 1967 to set up the University's first professional actor training programme. In 1970 he became Artistic Director of Seattle Repertory Theatre, leaving in 1979 for Los Angeles, where he was Dean of Theatre at the University of Southern California (USC) and continued working, not only as a teacher but also as a director and Hollywood actor, until shortly before his death, aged 68, in January 1987.

5. 1961-63 All change -
turn and turn again

Principal: Richard Ainley

Training at BOVTS was particularly confusing for students who joined the School in September 1961, as their two years were presided over by three different Principals: Duncan Ross for the first term, Richard Ainley for the middle four, and Nat Brenner for the last. Richard Ainley impressed the Bristol Old Vic Trust with his wealth of enthusiasm and ideas about acting, and arrived as Principal in November 1961, but stayed only four terms, until the spring of 1963, by which time many of the staff who had worked so closely with Duncan Ross had resigned, among them teachers Daphne Heard and Maggie Collins, and School Secretary Paula Gwyn-Davies.

Richard Ainley - an 'act-or' in the old-fashioned tradition of his famous father, Henry Ainley - had trained at the London Old Vic Theatre School and been acknowledged as one of Britain's leading young performers in the 1930s. But he had been badly injured in the 1940s when the jeep he was travelling in went over a landmine, and the severe disabilities he suffered worsened with the passing of time. In the early 1950s he was a visiting teacher at Rose Bruford College, where Douglas Dempster was among his students: 'We did scenes from *Hamlet,* and I found his ideas very unusual and very stimulating. He didn't like the idea of a pale, wan, Victorian, romantic Hamlet. He saw him as a lusty young man - because you can't be a wally in a world like that! We had a lot of girls in our groups, so he had the court packed with silly twittering females who were always waving handkerchiefs at the King, which made for a very funny scene instead of the usual dark and pompous atmosphere. It didn't have to be right; it didn't have to be valid - but it did stop you thinking along those old wooden lines. He influenced my thinking: when I read Shakespeare, I didn't think about dressing up, because we wore our ordinary clothes. He said our characters and authority came from within, it didn't consist in costumes.'

By the time Richard Ainley arrived at BOVTS, he was partially paralysed, walked with a limp, had a withered arm, a metal plate in his head, and a slight palsy in one side of his face. Despite these physical handicaps, and consequent frustrations, he was a likeable and charismatic man. John McEnery conjures an image of 'an enormous role model for Richard III'; Poppy Green (then known as Candida Fawsitt) recalls him as 'a man of overwhelming good humour, with a booming voice and a beaming smile'; and Gillian Barrington describes him as 'larger than life and rather strange. I imagine the old actor/managers must have been rather like him. I remember his declaiming from the balcony of the University Studio, when he didn't realise we were there. We thought he was a bit of a ham and found him hard to relate to. I think we resented him because he was so unlike Bill Ross.'

Richard Ainley was a disturbing contrast in style for the students who had spent their first year with Ross, because he didn't believe in the same kind of acting, or the way they had been doing plays: 'I suspect, looking back,' says Ruth Caleb, 'that Richard Ainley never had a chance. He was a traditionalist, part of an old theatrical establishment. Seeing students pretending to be teapots was as alien to him as going to Mars.'

From January 1962, Richard Ainley was joined by John Hodgson as Deputy Principal: 'It was wonderful for me, because Richard knew all about the theatre but knew nothing about teaching,' says John, who had taught and acted between taking a first degree at Durham and an MA at Oxford. 'So he gave me carte blanche with the syllabus, and I used to draw up the teaching programme with him. Rudi always did his Movement in the morning - we tried to make that the foundation of the work, and develop that into the Speech programme, the Singing programme, the Improvisation programme, the Text work and so on, developing it into more and more production work.'

During the short time that Richard Ainley and John Hodgson ran the School, they set up a new Directors' course (offering opportunities to sit in on London Old Vic rehearsals with Tyrone Guthrie and others) and made various small but significant improvements to the Downside Road buildings, including setting up a radio facility with a control room in the attic and microphones in various studio rooms: 'One of the things we recorded was *Hamlet* with Graham Haberfield playing Hamlet, and Richard himself as the Ghost of Hamlet's father.' After leaving Bristol in 1964, John Hodgson went to Bretton Hall, where he was for many years Professor of Performing Arts. David Goldsmith, who designed Hodgson's 1962 student production of *The Long and the Short and the Tall*, writes that 'I learnt from him about the theatre as a mirror on society. About using the theatre as an art form to shake the senses, to uncover hidden emotions, to lift the deepest, darkest aspects of life and place them before a live audience so that all could share a moment of truth'.

The eighteen months in Bristol were a difficult time for Richard Ainley, whose wife and children remained based in London where she had her practice as a doctor, while he lived in the flat at 2 Downside Road, sometimes with other members of the staff living in. His acute awareness of the unfavourable comparisons the second year students made between himself and Duncan Ross developed into something of a fixation. One of his contemporaries shivers to remember how 'He used to stomp around the School with his strange leg, intoning in a terrible, terrible voice, "The ghost of Dun-can Ross *leaves* me"'.

'Richard's health was failing, and he wasn't able to cope,' recalls Douglas Dempster, who joined his staff in October 1962 and was shocked by the change in him. 'I don't think people fully realised the sheer frustration of a man who had been exceptionally able, and who knew he was no longer able. When he raged, he had a huge voice, which could be heard all over the School. He was like a tethered bull, roaring in frustration and anger. But he could be such an endearing man, with a large chunk of the mischievous child in him.'

Douglas Dempster had left Rose Bruford in 1954 with a choice of skilled careers - as a dancer, a mime or a professional fencer. Instead he chose the theatre, and began his career as an electrician at the Edinburgh Festival, later working as an ASM, an actor, a designer and a director. During his twelve years at BOVTS, he taught acting, improvisation and later fencing as well as directing student productions: 'Nat Brenner used to say

I was the choreographer of the School, and give me huge casts of thirty actors for crowd scenes,' says Douglas, who left BOVTS at Christmas 1974 to teach at the Welsh College of Music and Drama. Students remember him for his open and 'non-interventional' style of teaching: 'He was great fun to work with because he was always more likely to say "What do you want to do?" than "Here's what you're going to do".'

As an actor, Richard Ainley believed in learning by doing, which meant he concentrated his considerable energies towards putting on more and more productions, both internal and public. The administration of the School began to falter: budgets were overspent; letters went unwritten or unanswered; auditions didn't happen. Debts mounted until they were more than the value of the Downside Road buildings, and the School was faced with a real possibility of having to close down.

During the tribute event to launch the Nat Brenner Scholarship Fund in November 1993, Professor Glynne Wickham, who was on the Management Committees of both the Company and the School in the early 1960s, described how Nat came to be invited to take over the School, revealing how the end finally came for Richard Ainley: 'Being the fine actor that he had been, he consoled his spirits from time to time with practical jokes, and some of these lifted his spirits. Some of them caused a considerable deal of laughter for all concerned. Others however were not so well received by students, staff, or the governors. This matter came to a head one winter's evening when, very lonely, he thought time might pass more quickly if he were to be accompanied by some convivial companion to share a conversation over a bottle of Scotch. So he phoned up a chum. Inexplicably, his choice landed upon the Chairman of the School Sub-Committee, an aged alderman. Picking up the phone, it occurred to him that some disguise was needed to excuse this call. What should it be? Rape - that would fetch him. Perfect. So. The worthy alderman, awoken at 1am, to his very great credit jumped in his car, and went straight to the School. There he was doubly affronted, first to discover that there had been no rape. Second, that, as a lifelong temperance worker, he was presented with a bottle of Scotch which he was expected to consume before dawn. Enough was enough. The governors, regretfully, agreed.'

Richard Ainley continued to work as an actor until his death in May 1967, at the age of 56: 'We were cast by Bernard Miles in *The Trojan Wars* at the Mermaid Theatre,' writes Poppy Green, who had played Cleopatra when she was a student at BOVTS. 'The moment Richard saw me his rich tones sounded across the stage, "My little Cleopatra!" Richard was playing the old, war-wounded hero Tyndarius, a part for which he was ideal, both because of his disability and his acting skills. Watching Richard as an actor in rehearsals, I gleaned some measure of how brilliant he would have been in performance; but this was not to be. One morning I arrived at the stage door, with a note from Richard I had received in the post still in my hand: "Dear Cleopatra," it read, "I know money is in short supply (we were all receiving £11 a week) so here's a bit to help out. Don't spend it all on cigs. Richard." Enclosed was a crumpled ten shilling note. The stage door keeper told me the sad news that Richard had died during the night, while sitting up late studying his lines.'

2. First BOV Theatre School Director Edward Stanley, on stage with Edith Manvell in a BOVTS production of G B Shaw's *The Man of Destiny.*

1. The 'fruit school' at 27 Queen Charlotte Street.

3. Hugh Hunt, first Director of the BOV Company, talks to Theatre School students at Queen Charlotte Street.

4. A fencing class at Queen Charlotte Street with Rudi Shelly.

5. One of the School's first end-of-year productions, in the Theatre Royal, 1947: *The Insect Play* by Karel and Josef Capek.

6. Two of the School's first students, John Dalby and Rita McKerrow.

7. Edward Stanley, Director
of the Bristol Old Vic
Theatre School 1946-1954.

8. and **9.** BOVTS students in the
courtyards of Saint Nicholas School,
opposite the 'fruit school' in Queen
Charlotte Street.

10. Class of 1951-52 outside Saint Nicholas School : Director Edward
Stanley (sitting, centre); Assistant Director Anthony Holland (standing, far
left); Bursar Jack Moss (standing, fourth from right) Rudi Shelly (standing,
far right); Edith Manvell (sitting, second from right); students pictured
include Kenneth Cope, Pat Heywood, Joan Knight, Phyllida Law, Roy
Skelton, Julian Slade, Mary Steele, Antony Tuckey, and Elizabeth West.

11. BOVTS production of *Everyman* (University Drama Studio, 1954).

12. Duncan 'Bill' Ross,
Principal of the Bristol
Old Vic Theatre School
1954-1961.

13. Duncan Ross with students at Downside Road.

14. On stage with Peter O'Toole in the BOV Company's spring 1958 production of *The Pier*: BOVTS students made up the crowd of rebellious teenagers.

15. Richard Ainley, BOVTS Principal 1961-1963, watches students prepare for a 1962 production of Willis Hall's *The Long and The Short and The Tall* at the Artillery Ground in Whiteladies Road.

6. 1963-80 From each according to their abilities, to each according to their needs

Principal: Nat Brenner

The early 1960s were a time of significant change for the Bristol Old Vic. In 1961 Laurence Olivier had been invited to take over the Old Vic Theatre in London's Waterloo Road and install his company there as the National Theatre of Great Britain. As one consequence of this, the London Old Vic Company was wound up in 1963, and the Bristol Old Vic Company became a fully independent organisation with its own Board of Governors. Something had to be done about the School.

Nat Brenner became the new Principal a few months before President Kennedy was assassinated, and steered his students on a determinedly classical and traditional course through the turbulent years of mid-1960s' Beatlemania, late 1960s' political protest and hippie flower power, early 1970s' ostentatious glam-rock glitter, and later 1970s' punk rebellion, resigning as Principal soon after Margaret Thatcher was elected Prime Minister.

Nat was a man with a precise grasp of economic reality as well as artistic quality. It's been said of him that he could look at a theatre set and accurately price it to the nearest penny. Yet, reveals his Technical Director Roger Jeffery, 'During Nat's regime, there never was a fixed budget for productions - which may surprise some people. He would say to me "Spend what is reasonably necessary to do a proper job". But he did have a coded way of letting me know if he thought I'd overspent. He would call me into the office a month or two later when the invoices came in and make me go through them in detail!'

When Richard Ainley left in the spring of 1963, Nat Brenner initially took on responsibility for the School alongside his existing duties as General Manager of the Company. By the autumn of 1963, Douglas Morris had been appointed to take over as BOV General Manager and Nat Brenner was confirmed as Principal of the School, which by careful management and dedicated effort he soon restored to a viable financial footing. It was a timely move, for Nat was unhappy about the changes which Val May had begun making to the Bristol Old Vic Company since becoming Artistic Director in 1961. Nat wanted it to stay as it was, fulfilling his evangelical dream of what a regional theatre should be. But Val May was determined to steer the BOV on a policy of expansion: in 1963 he took on a second stage, the Little Theatre; in 1970-72 he oversaw the radical rebuilding that created the New Vic Studio and completely changed everything around and about the Theatre Royal except the appearance of the auditorium; and for fourteen years he took BOV productions to London and all over the world.

By the time Nat Brenner became Principal of BOVTS, he'd already had experience in every aspect of the business: he had acted with the Arts Council's Midland Theatre Company in the 1940s; he could sing and dance; he'd been a stage manager; and he'd done everything from designing and rigging lighting to running his own theatre. Nat was an extraordinary individual, a fiercely intelligent, really rounded theatrical person who inspired lasting respect for his professional achievements as well as for his remarkable knowledge and ability as a teacher - and a sense of humour frequently described as 'wicked'.

In November 1993, the School launched a Nat Brenner Scholarship Fund with a tribute show at Bristol's Theatre Royal called *To Nat At 6.30,* produced and performed by a star-studded company of his grateful ex-students. Devised by Anthony Falkingham, it was directed by John Caird, with lighting by Wayne Dowdeswell and sound by John Leonard; there were scenes from Shaw and Wilde, featuring Annette Crosbie, Ian Gelder, Jeremy Irons, Alex Jennings, Jane Lapotaire, Tim Pigott-Smith and Amanda Redman; Jeremy Child and Richard Howard sang *Strollin'* together; there were solo songs from Samantha Bond, David Calder, Jeremy Irons, Aled Jones, Louise Plowright, Jenny Seagrove and John Telfer; and contributions from Brendan O'Hea, Mark Lambert, Miranda Richardson, Joanna Riding, Marc Sinden, Julian Slade, Trudie Styler and Kit Thacker, with a musical chorus of current students.

'That evening was so representative of Nat,' says Jane Lapotaire. 'It drew a really vivid picture of him: his whisky drinking, his communism, the fact that he was a visionary. No-one could ever overestimate the influence that man had on those of us who were lucky enough to pass through his hands. Not just the impressive names like Greta Scacchi and Daniel Day-Lewis and Jeremy Irons - Nat was responsible for three generations of youngsters going into the theatre. And he was a great purist, and a traditionalist, and a lover of Shaw and of well-spoken English and good grammar. He was our mentor, our teacher, our friend, our guide. To me, he was a surrogate dad, and like a grandfather to my son.'

Margaret Courtenay recalled working during the war in the ABCA (Army Bureau of Current Affairs) Play Unit with Nat, who was then a Battery Sergeant Major in the Royal Artillery. They toured 'living newspaper plays - daily script changes and a travelling set in two lorries, all masterminded by Nat, who was not only the Company Manager, but also lit the show, acted in it, and blithely laughed and cursed his way from one Army unit to the next.'

David Calder paid tribute to Nat as a committed socialist, recalling many nights both as a student and later, when 'we would stay up until the early hours of the morning with the inevitable bottle of whisky, putting to rights the wrongs of the world'. Calder, who was at the time playing Shylock with the RSC at Stratford, also offered an insight into that production's approach to the anti-Semitism inherent in *The Merchant of Venice,* navigating a line through the play that allowed Shylock to come over as a respectable man of business and an upright figure of the community. During the discussions, Calder had insisted that there was no need to be sentimental about it, because 'I know that you'll find unsentimental attitudes coming from Jewish people - and of course the Jewish person I had in mind was Nat Brenner. When I did the play some years before this, I remember him saying to me, "You know, the one thing to remember, when you play Shylock, is that he is a twenty-four carat gold **shit**"!' Though born into a Jewish family, Nat was not a believer in any religion, and responded to students' complaints about working on Saturdays with a terse 'What is it - the Sabbath?'

His career had begun with London's left-wing Unity Theatre before the war, and he met his wife Joan, an actress then serving as an ATS Sergeant, while on attachment to the Army Play Unit. In the late 1940s, he worked at Salisbury Arts Theatre with Denis Carey, with whom he came to Bristol when Carey became Director of the BOV Company: 'In 1950 I had a choice,' Nat told the BOV Theatre Club in 1986, 'I was offered the job of Artistic Director if I stayed (at Salisbury) or I could join the Bristol Old Vic as Production Manager. Less money, and it wasn't the road I really wished to travel. But the lure of that theatre, the Theatre Royal, Bristol, coupled with the standards, aims and reputation of the Bristol Old Vic was too much, just too seductive ... It seemed to me then that it (Bristol) was the sort of provincial city which offered the chance to meet the Utopian dream of a theatre as the focus, the centre for the social, the artistic and the intellectual stimulus of a community. To quote Bernard Shaw: "A Temple of the Ascent of Man"; as well as a place of entertainment.'

As Production Manager from 1950 to 1959, Nat had an office in what had been Sarah Siddons' dressing room at the Theatre Royal; from 1959 to 1963, he was General Manager of the BOV Company. Throughout his lifelong association with the Bristol Old Vic, he occasionally directed plays not only with the School but also for the Company, notably *Plunder* with his great friend Peter O'Toole in 1973. It was thanks to Nat Brenner that Peter O'Toole, who trained at RADA, began his career with the Bristol Old Vic in 1955, making his professional debut at the Theatre Royal as a cab driver in *The Matchmaker*. Nat had been very impressed by the young O'Toole, but knew that the BOV didn't need - and couldn't afford - any more actors at that time. Nevertheless he persuaded Director John Moody to see this one, and even arranged a cut in his own pay so that the Company would take him on. A frequent visitor to Downside Road between the 1950s and 1970s, Peter O'Toole helped the School in various ways, from giving scholarships to pay for students' training to arranging and paying for all the final year actors and techies to go to Shepperton, where they watched him filming and were taken round the Studios.

Twenty-five years later, School Secretary Erika Neumann still vividly remembers starting work at BOVTS: 'It was the first of March, the middle of a term, and Nat was in rehearsal for a play. People were ringing up, and the only thing I was told was never *ever* to interrupt Nat Brenner while he was rehearsing. Unless it was Peter O'Toole. In which case, go and fetch him. On my second day, who should phone up but Peter O'Toole! I couldn't find the rehearsal studio to start with, because it's a rambling building, and there was no-one around. When I found the studio I knocked on the door - no reply. Knocked again - no reply. Walked in. Nat didn't turn round. All the students turned round and looked at me. Nat was quite intimidating to the students in those days, though he had a heart of gold, and when I got to know him he was the most lovely man ever. No-one said anything, and eventually I had to say "Excuse me, Mr Brenner" - "Yes!" he snapped - "It's Mr O'Toole on the telephone" - "Oh, right darling!" and up he comes!'

Erika Neumann has been a friend to generations of actors since she joined the Bristol Old Vic Theatre School in 1971: 'There was far less work in those days. It was very laid back, we had far more time and we used to entertain the students in the office, have a cup of coffee, and sit and have a chat. Whereas now there's not a hope in hell of doing that, we're far too busy! We made coffee only twice a day in those days, a ritual that I inherited from the previous Secretary, Maria Moller, who was very disciplined and of the old school. She would only have tea and coffee at the proper times, namely 11.15 and 3.15.'

Though the staff now drink tea whenever they like, Erika still maintains a strong sense of discipline in the office: 'I don't suffer fools gladly, and I don't mind if you say so! I love the students dearly and there's nothing I wouldn't do for them, but I won't stand any nonsense because with a hundred students in the School we can't afford to. Some of them will probably have stories to tell - Stephen Dillane, who's done very well since, assures me he was the only student I ever sacked from the School cleaning job.'

'I felt that it was unfair dismissal,' says Mr Dillane. 'But Erika is not to be argued with - and getting sacked is my claim to fame at the School!'

Nat Brenner has countless claims to fame at the School, among them his caustic, acerbic wit, and his colourful language when teaching and directing. 'He had relish, in the way he bit out words. He had a wonderful way with a one-liner,' recalls one admirer, remembering a time when Nat was very frustrated by the way women in his classes walked: because they often wore trousers in everyday life, they took strides too long for the historical style of the practice skirts they were wearing. 'He would say "Look darling, imagine you've got a clove of garlic up your fanny and Dracula's after you", and after that the girls would keep their legs much closer together, and walk in the right style!'

Errant students risked being asked to leave the class with a typically pointed remark: 'You like sex? You like travel? Well, fuck off!' But he never swore in normal conversation or in front of his children, and told his daughters that swearing showed a poverty of vocabulary.

Nat was a chain-smoker, and flamboyant with it. Former students picture him cross-legged on a chair, cigarette in his mouth, with an enormous gravity-defying length of ash on it. Many cheerfully describe his bit of well-practised business with a cigarette, which could hold the attention of his class for nearly an hour: he would take a filter tip cigarette, and tap it on the table a few times, then put it in his mouth, unlit for a disturbingly long time, occasionally taken out of his mouth and put in again, apparently distracted, often the wrong way round; several times he would repeat the process of taking a match from the box, eventually striking it, but then letting it burn down to his fingers. David Henry Salter believes he was the only student who ever had the courage to tell Nat he was about to light the filter tip. John Hartoch remembers one hilarious lesson when Nat had been tapping the cigarette as usual - then went to write with it on the chalkboard.

Though Nat gave up smoking when he was diagnosed with bronchial asthma in the early 1980s, he already had the emphysema which contributed to his death, but possibly also helped to give his voice the distinctive nicotine-soaked sound that Jack Klaff compares to 'a drum full of toffees rolling down a hill'.

He was the sort of man who could command silence in a room just by entering it. John McEnery remembers him as 'very austere in contrast to Richard Ainley, a dour and rather disturbing presence who left students awe struck'. Many students admit to being not just in awe but actually frightened of Nat, even after many years' acquaintance. Though he had an unfailing eye for feminine beauty, some say he lacked a certain gentle touch with the girls, who could find his carefully cultivated 'man of the theatre' image quite overbearing.

Yet there are stories suggesting that he had a fine sense of fun, and deliberately cut a terrifying figure so as to impress on students the respect for discipline that is so important for theatre workers. Jack Klaff recalls what happened after David Mallinson, Annabel Rosier and Heida Steindors missed a day at the School because they went for a walk that turned into something of an expedition, ending up on a beach in Wales: 'David was determined to tell Nat the truth, so he said "It was very romantic, a lovely night", this and that, the whole story, ending up on the beach, and Nat said "Hmm, missed a day, a whole day, hmm, very important work" and he wagged this very important finger at them, then said "Next time - take me with you". I think that sums him up.'

If Nat admitted to any religion at all, it was Punctuality: 'I used to be known as "cut-it-fine Irons", because I never liked getting to places early,' confesses Oscar-winner Jeremy. 'The deal was that we had to be at School before Nat was. I remember walking up Pembroke Road towards the School and seeing Nat on the far pavement and I'd increase my stride to try to overtake him without him noticing, and as I increased my stride, he obviously *had* noticed me because he would increase his stride, and the strides would get longer and longer until the first one broke into a bit of a run, and finally the two of us were haring up the road trying to beat each other to work, this fifty-year old man and eighteen-year-old student, who liked each other very much.'

Jeremy Child 'was one of the privileged few who used to go up and spend time with Nat and Joan in the flat. I could listen to him talking for hours on end about theatre, performances, Shakespeare, Chekhov, Shaw'. Many remember joining Nat in Clifton's Alma Tavern, where his favoured tipple was pints of Guinness, though he was also partial to what he called 'Scottish water', be it Bell's, Teacher's, or a good malt.

For as long as Nat was willing to talk, students were

always ready to listen, even late into the night when he gave notes in the Theatre Royal auditorium after dress rehearsals for a production: 'He didn't seem to notice the time, sometimes it would be one or two in the morning, but nobody complained, because his notes were always brilliant - sharp, succinct, to the point, and so interesting and instructive.'

For the first seven years, the Brenner family - Nat, Joan, and their daughters Ruth and Susie - lived in the flat at 2 Downside Road, with a sitting room and kitchen on the first floor and bedrooms at the top of the house: 'Joan was as much a part of the School's life as Nat was,' says Jane Lapotaire. 'She had the most wonderful husky voice. And if you'd got half an hour to spare you could pop upstairs and have a gin and tonic and a quick cigarette with Joan, and a bit of motherly advice and a cuddle, and a damn good laugh!'

Nat soon persuaded the Bristol Old Vic Trust of the need for additional rehearsal space, and in 1966 funds were found to build, on the Downfield Road side of the School, a New Rehearsal Studio (long referred to as the 'NRS'), a 1,350 square foot space which can also comfortably seat a hundred people for in-house performances. The link between Theatre School and Company remained strong, with students often sent down to King Street to do walk-on parts, unpaid in term time, but given 'expenses' if the show went into the School holidays: 'We learnt a lot from the experienced actors, who then included Dorothy Tutin, Frank Middlemass and Peter Vaughan,' recalls Richard Frost, 'and we not only appeared eight times a week but also did an all-night fit-up from Saturday night through to Monday afternoon on the show we were in.'

The class of 1967-69 were as enthusiastic about being in the auditorium as on the stage: Christopher Biggins and Jacqueline Stanbury started a First Night Club, when all the students would dress up in black tie or long dresses to attend performances in the Theatre Royal, where Theatre Manager Rodney West always reserved the best available seats for them. There was clearly a special relationship as well as an abundance of talent: six 1969 graduates were taken straight into the Company, among them Jeremy Irons, Simon Cadell, and Tim Pigott-Smith, who was also a graduate from the University Drama Department.

Under Nat Brenner and Glynne Wickham there was a degree of cross-fertilisation between the Theatre School and the University, even though some student actors failed to appreciate the value of the academic perspective - and equally as many University students had little time for the vocational approach. Two large celebrations in the mid-1960s engaged the enthusiasm of all three sides of the 'Bristol triangle', with contributions from the University as well as the BOV Company and Theatre School for the 1964 Shakespeare Quatercentenary and the 1966 bicentenary of the Theatre Royal.

In 1967, when the Drama Department moved to Cantocks Close, the derelict Vandyck printing works was converted into a new studio theatre. Whereas the Wills Building Drama Studio had been twenty-eight feet wide, the Vandyck building had concrete floors dotted at twenty-foot intervals with metal pillars, which the architect insisted were structurally impossible to remove. Could they build a theatre round the pillars? Nat Brenner was consulted. 'Impossible,' he said. The pillars came out. The Vandyck Theatre (since re-named the Wickham Theatre in honour of Professor Glynne Wickham, who retired in 1982) was officially opened on 19 March 1968 by Princess Marina (then Patron of the BOV Trust) and continued to host Theatre School productions until the early 1980s.

As the School developed, needing more and more space, it became impractical for the Principal to live on the premises and the Brenners moved out to a house in Aberdeen Road, Redland. Their bay-windowed drawing room became a technical studio, and Nat's bedroom became a studio for the middle year of a new three-year Acting course originally designed to allow younger actors to explore their developing personalities as well as their professional skills. For its first four years, between 1970 and 1974, special responsibility for this intermediate year of training lay with David Henry Salter, who had taken a degree in Drama and French at Bristol University before training as an actor at the Theatre School. He had worked for 'two exciting years of innovative ensemble theatre at the newly-formed Everyman Theatre in Liverpool', then six months in a Pitlochry Festival season directed by Chris Denys before being invited back to Bristol by Nat Brenner.

'The students continued their Voice and Movement

classes with the others,' writes Mr Salter, 'but the core of their sandwich year was as a small ensemble group, a private company almost, which lived and worked and played in its own little studio. We rarely performed our creations for the other students or in theatres, but took them out into the community, to schools or hospitals or workplaces, non-traditional performance areas. Not all the work was free-form or improvised, although the BBC took some interest in that side of our work and created several broadcast radio dramas based on it.'

After David Henry Salter left Bristol in 1974 to become a Senior Lecturer in the Drama Department of the Flinders University of South Australia, his place was taken by Anthony Falkingham, who stayed until December 1978. He too had trained at BOVTS, after working as a young actor at Bradford Civic Playhouse and being an Equity £1-a-week student ASM at Birmingham's Old Rep in the early 1960s.

By the end of the 1970s, Roger Jeffery had commandeered three rooms for use as technical studios, including the former library (now a video room) on the first floor of 1 Downside Road. He also converted a kitchen and bathroom into a photographic darkroom and a small sound editing suite, and gradually colonised most of the attic as a Wardrobe workroom and store, which it remains to this day.

In 1975, when Val May moved to Guildford's Yvonne Arnaud Theatre, Richard Cottrell took over as Artistic Director of the BOV Company, continuing the long-established tradition of using student actors in walk-on parts, and taking new BOVTS graduates into the Company, which in 1978 was presenting plays on three stages, and had a regular company of thirty-five actors on its books. John Telfer went straight from the School into the Company, and worked for them often in his first five years: 'Richard Cottrell gave me every break under the sun, never typecast me in anything, put me in all sorts of different stuff, and gave me better and better parts. It was the best possible start, working with the great actors who were there then - Harold Innocent, Daniel Massey, Jane Lapotaire, Pete Postlethwaite. It was the sort of post-Theatre School training that young actors don't get now because they're always put on such short contracts.'

Nat often encouraged ex-students to return to the School

to share and develop their skills. Richard Howard, who has frequently directed BOVTS student productions - including most of the summer showcases in the New Vic since 1985 - worked as an actor in the theatre for ten years, 'almost constantly, in all the big reps, the Royal Court and the National, with bits of TV,' then came back to Bristol in the mid-1970s as 'a sort of golf pro in the theatre', taking Text classes with students, acting in some trainee directors' productions, and staging his own Fringe work within the School.

Both the staff and the students were fired by Nat Brenner's passionate belief in the theatre, and his well-developed appreciation of every theatrical style. Nat himself was particularly inspired by the great socialist playwright George Bernard Shaw, whose ideals he shared and whose works he loved to read and to produce. As a teacher, he also shared the ideals of the London Old Vic, as he outlined in a 1992 radio interview:

'The Old Vic School in London was a marvellous school, run by three great men of the theatre - Michel Saint-Denis, Glen Byam Shaw and George Devine, who put their hearts and soul into the idea of a great school in preparation for a National Theatre - the Old Vic then - so that the best of training could be offered. Though it was forced to close, the influence of it on me, and on the classical training, and on the people I met who were graduates from that School, when they came to the Bristol Old Vic, so impressed me - the way they rehearsed, and the way they worked on a part - that I decided I would try and do what we could here, in the image and inspiration of the Old Vic School, London. Of course we couldn't do anything like that, because we couldn't afford it. But we worked on the principle of a classical training, serving and providing the repertory companies in those days - who were in excellent form, not the fragmented commercial-seeking organisations that take place now ... it was all post-war idealism and renaissance and all that. The idea was that we would be able to provide from the Theatre School people who could play in the best of plays, and do those plays *great*. But of course it has been modified by expediency and common sense - the advent of television introduced new modes. So the School has mutated a little, but the principles of providing the best thing we can, and the dedication, are still there.'

Nat firmly believed that an actor who could work effectively on the classics was capable of adapting to anything. Throughout the changes of the 1960s and 1970s, when an increasing number of performers were finding work in television and on the Fringe as well as in the regional theatres, he maintained that his primary purpose was to cultivate 'classical' actors as potential for the leading repertory companies.

From the early 1960s through to the mid-1970s, the core team of teachers at BOVTS remained the same: Rudi Shelly, ever in revolt against specialisation, teaching not only Movement but everything an actor would find it useful to know; Lynn Britt taking on the more energetic aspects of Dance and Movement; Douglas Dempster giving Improvisation and Fencing classes, and directing productions; John Oxley for Singing; Katy Stafford for Voice and Speech; Roger Jeffery in charge of the Technical courses.

The complex timetable was managed for twenty-five years by Associate Principal Adrian Cairns, who joined the School in the autumn of 1964, after helping to set up Tyne-Tees Television in Newcastle-upon-Tyne. Arriving on his first day, he found the Principal, sleeves rolled up, with a heavy duty bucket and mop, cleaning the floor of the Movement studio. 'Can I help?' he asked, cautiously. 'No,' Nat replied, 'not unless you need the therapy.' Trained as an actor at the London Old Vic Theatre School, Adrian Cairns worked mainly in television, where he was well known as a presenter and can still be seen occasionally in cameo roles as judges and suchlike, suiting his 'old-fashioned, gentle, gentlemanly manner'. As well as his administrative responsibilities, he directed numerous Theatre School productions and took classes in Text and Acting exercises. He had a particular talent for reducing classic plays to one scene: one of his groups did the whole of *She Stoops to Conquer* in an hour, recalls Marion Reed, who played Mrs Hardcastle to Christopher Biggins' Tony Lumpkin.

Since Adrian Cairns retired in 1989, responsibility for the timetable has been taken over by Elwyn Johnson, who joined the full time staff in 1979, as did BOVTS-trained John Hartoch, who had recently worked with Elwyn at Lancaster

Rep. Nat himself retired from full time work in 1980 to spend more time with his wife Joan, who had suffered with Parkinson's disease since the late 1960s. After her death in 1981, he came back to the Bristol Old Vic, teaching at the School and making one rare appearance as an actor, playing Brovik in Paul Unwin's 1989 Theatre Royal production of *The Master Builder*. As it became clear that his own health was failing, several people suggested that Nat should write about his life and his ideas, but he never got round to it. He was essentially a talker, not a writer. Blessed with a most fantastic memory, he'd never felt the need to write things down. He never forgot a student or an actor, and could always recall all their names - and a great deal about their careers too. In his last few years Nat lived with his daughter Susie and her family in Cardiff, teaching masterclasses at the Welsh College of Music and Drama, 'very pleased to still be making a contribution', and returning regularly to the Bristol Old Vic Theatre School until six weeks before his death at the age of 77 on 14 April 1993.

7. 1980-96 Onward, ever onward - meeting new challenges

Principal: Christopher Denys

Christopher Denys was Nat Brenner's own choice to take over as Principal of the Bristol Old Vic Theatre School: 'I took it on as a very clear responsibility to keep it the way Nat had made it - by which I mean to keep it changing, and in touch with what is happening. Since I've been here, the changes in the profession have been more extreme and more varied than at any other time in the forty-odd years I've been in the business,' says Chris, who started in theatre at the age of twelve as stage crew, follow-spot and bucket-scrubber before becoming a full time skater and dancer at fifteen, then an actor in rep and on tour. After National Service as an Army bandsman, he returned to acting, also working in TV and radio, and began directing in the mid-1950s 'when rep theatre still offered plays twice nightly with a weekly changeover'.

In 1961, he came to Bristol Old Vic from Nottingham Playhouse with Val May, first as Company Stage Manager, then Production Manager, then Associate Director until 1967. He has been Artistic Director at Worthing Connaught Theatre, Pitlochry Festival Theatre, Basilica Opera and the Royal Theatre and Opera House, Northampton. Before becoming Principal of BOVTS in 1980, he worked for eight years as a freelance director and playwright, and has continued writing and directing outside the School. For Radio 4, he has sixteen plays, numerous adaptations and several series and documentaries to his credit. These allow him to keep in touch with the gossip - 'who's doing what, what's coming up, who's casting' - without taking him away from the School for very long: 'When you write for radio, they either like it or they don't. You don't have to spend a lot of time beyond the writing process - it's just a few days in the studios, none of the sitting down with a committee that's part of writing for television, or attending rehearsals in the theatre,' says Chris, who is a former Chairman of the Drama Panel of South West Arts and has also worked widely as a theatre consultant for regional theatres and local authorities.

The early 1980s were a time of radical change in British economic and social policies, as what would later be called 'Thatcherism' transformed public services into commercial enterprises and tried to replace arts subsidy with business sponsorship. Within a few years, the activities of the regional theatres were severely curtailed, and it was less and less likely that most of the Bristol Old Vic Theatre School graduates would be able to consolidate their training with the sort of first job that offered several months of working alongside experienced professionals. Chris Denys responded to the increasingly pragmatic demands of the modern 'industry' by preparing the students not only classically but also commercially, instilling in them a very practical and businesslike approach: 'Acting is a job. You have to do the adverts, the voice-overs or whatever, or you won't still be a working actor when the chance to do "the art" comes along.'

The change in attitude also brought some significant changes of staff: dancer and choreographer Aubrey Budd was Head of Movement from 1981 until 1984, when Gail Gordon took on that role. Neil Rhoden became the School's first full time Musical Director in the spring of 1983. That summer Technical Director Roger Jeffery resigned, to be replaced by Cliff Zenker, then by Paul Rummer, who has been Head of Technical Courses since 1985, with a gradually enlarged team of teachers to meet the demands of a two year course and ever-changing technologies and working practices. Among the expanded part time staff was June Burrough, a former BOV Company Stage Manager, who taught jobsearch and management skills to the Technical students and later employed BOVTS-trained actors for role-playing workshops in business, for example giving managers practice in dealing with difficult human situations such as serving redundancy notices or following disciplinary procedures.

Tackling the increasing need to offer realistic work experience in radio and television as well as live theatre has also meant lengthening the Theatre School day, and although there are no Saturday morning sessions (to allow students to take paid jobs at weekends), weekday working now begins with limbers at 8.30am and ends at 7.15pm rather than 5.15pm: 'We are, after all, still trying to give students understanding and practical experience of two and a half thousand years of playwriting,' says Chris Denys. 'We are still determined to concentrate on "classical" texts in the conviction that if you can get your head and your mouth round Shakespeare, most other things are comparatively straightforward.'

There's a clear and constant pattern to the style of playtexts used in training, though the titles chosen vary from year to year depending on the strengths and weaknesses of each particular group. In a recent and typical year, first year Acting students worked in the classroom (on their feet) on the full texts of *The Man of Mode, Macbeth, The School for Scandal, Romeo and Juliet, The Apple Cart* and *After Liverpool* together with further scenes from Shakespeare, selections of scenes ranging from the Greek plays to Restoration, and excerpts from *Hay Fever, Private Lives, Present Laughter*, and the plays of Tom Stoppard, David Hare, C P Taylor, Alan Ayckbourn and Alan Bennett.

In the same year, second year students worked in the classroom on *The Cherry Orchard* and two separate television projects (one on location and one in the studio) while performing three shows in public: *The Nativity* in schools, churches and hospitals; *Hiawatha* in local primary schools; and *Under Milk Wood* in twenty-two venues ranging from large, fully equipped theatres to village halls throughout the West Country.

Meanwhile, final year students worked in the classroom on *King Lear* and a television project, recorded productions of *As You Like It* and *Pride and Prejudice* for transmission on BBC local radio and performed eleven shows in public: *The Mysteries, Hard Times* and Peter Barnes' *Red Noses* at the New Vic; *Alice Through the Looking Glass* and *Love's Labour's Lost* at the Redgrave Theatre; *Mansfield Park* at the Theatre Royal; *The Jungle Book* at the RSC's Swan Theatre, Stratford-upon-Avon; *The Rehearsal, Mistero Buffo* and *Losers* as lunchtime shows in the New Vic Foyer; and *Cowardy Custard* as a late-nighter at the Theatre Royal.

Such is the passion of the students that many find the

time and energy and resourcefulness to put on their own extra-curricular productions as well. They're always busy, often working on several different projects at the same time: 'I had to learn to juggle for *Red Noses*,' says Christopher Mellows, 'and you don't just juggle balls here, it's juggling commitments and priorities too.' Countless actors and technicians who have been working in the business for years say it's never as hard as that again.

To a large extent what happens to students at Bristol Old Vic Theatre School depends on their own resources and responses: 'It's essentially a very personal training,' says Chris Denys. 'We deliberately keep the groups small, and just as deliberately we have no single preferred philosophy or style of teaching. Though there's a clear core syllabus of practical technique and factual information that has to be put across, beyond that we're working with individuals, trying to equip each one with whatever they need to make best use of whatever talent they have, and taking account of their personality, their background and their future prospects in the profession. It's up to them to decide what they want to do with their lives - all the options are here, but they have to make the selection and discovery.'

'Nowadays no-one can get by on doing only one form of theatre,' adds Elwyn Johnson, who has been Associate Principal (Acting Courses) since 1989. 'So we have to give them as many different experiences as possible, and say to them "There it all is, that's the game plan, you choose". Every acting student has to do everything: every style of theatre from musicals to Shakespeare, practice in front of a microphone and a camera, stage combat, everything - because you never know what's going to come in useful.'

Says Donalh MacNeil, who became Bath Theatre Royal's first full time Youth Theatre Director in 1994: 'Bristol gives you so many types and levels of skill and expertise that you're launched off into the business with a huge shove - into the deep end, but with the biggest parachute possible!'

Before Chris Denys came to Bristol, he had worked as an actor with people who had trained there under Edward Stanley and Duncan Ross: 'They were passionately serious about what they did, even if it was a funny part, and approached it through processes inside themselves which had been fostered and developed at the Bristol Old Vic School. When I joined the BOV Company as an Associate Director in the 1960s, I became aware of the School as being quite special and very much related to the job we were all doing down the road in King Street. When I left Bristol and ran theatres elsewhere, I found myself coming back as a potential employer. Of course I went to all the other drama schools as well, but I found that the enormous difference at that time - the late 1960s through to the middle 1970s - was that however well trained they were, the other students didn't really have an understanding of what the job was, whereas the students who came out of this School under Nat Brenner already had the attitudes that are required in the profession.

'When I was asked to take over the School, I was aware that I was taking over a professional organisation that had always been closely related to the industry for which it was training people. I use the word "industry", because that's what it is. Some of the jobs people go on to from here are artistically inspired and satisfying, but there's not enough of that kind of work to pay the rent.

'In glorious moments, it is "art", but only on very rare occasions. It's now a very wide industry, it's television, commercials, trade shows, voice-overs, radio, film - and, of course, theatre, which could be almost anything from West End to touring round church halls in an old van. For actors particularly, but for technicians as well, you have to be very good at making the bottom line living so that then you have some freedom of choice to develop your career.'

Marc Sinden admits to a similarly hard-nosed attitude towards acting as a business: 'I have to put my children through school, I've a house to keep, cars to run. It is a vocational trade, but when it comes down to it, you've got to eat,' he insists. 'Never mind art for art's sake - give me money for God's sake!'

Chris Denys expands on this theme: 'No-one can afford to build a career on working for the regional theatres, exciting as it is, because it can't pay enough money. So you have to be good at getting the money in the bank to be able to afford to work for even the RSC or the National. It's easier when you first go out, because you can just about survive on the Equity minimum, and everything you do is valuable. But ten years out, you need to be developing and growing into bigger and better parts, flexing your muscles with new things all through your working life. The work that excites people and keeps them in the profession is very often not very well paid, so they have to subsidise it. We hope they'll all have very high aspirations and want to be great actors playing great parts in great plays, but we have to prepare them for all aspects of the industry. The core training is the same, whatever medium the students are going to work in: whether they do radio, theatre, television, films - or, more likely, a combination of all of them - the basics they learn here are just as relevant.'

Greg Doran was one of the first intake of Acting students after Chris Denys took over: 'Nat regarded acting as a craft, and believed that if you knew your craft then you'd get on in the profession. Having much more practical experience of the professional theatre, and knowing how much harder it had become, Chris's approach is that you have to know your craft, but there's no point in knowing it unless you also know how to approach your career as a professional business. The criticism that was levelled against him was that there was too much performing and not enough training, which is a difficult argument, but what Chris was also doing differently from Nat was preparing people for the profession *as it is* - so he was trying to give people as many different kinds of experience as possible, including doing musicals. Suddenly all the Bristol Old Vic students could sing and dance, which they weren't really required to do before.'

'If they're good enough at music, there's a lot of work about,' says Chris, 'but even if they still sound like frogs they'll be able to hold a harmony line, and music develops the ear for speech-rhythms and cadences. Only some of them will be good enough to dance for ready money but *all* of them will be fitter, better co-ordinated, more physically expressive and better able to cope with the demands made on actors these days - a lot of running, vaulting over things, looking tough and any amount of fighting!'

There had been elementary radio facilities in the University Drama Studio, and at Downside Road, but in 1981 an arrangement was made with BBC Radio Bristol and its then General Manager, Derek Woodcock, for Theatre School students to work with BBC staff in professional studios to record two plays each year. The texts are chosen from the current secondary school syllabus, one a full-length Shakespeare, the other a play or dramatisation of a novel. They were directed in the early years by Brian Miller (who continued to teach basic radio technique) and later by Shaun MacLoughlin, and broadcast on an increasing number of BBC local radio stations just before the exams. In 1987, actors from the Theatre School also worked with BBC Radio Bristol's Vicki Klein on *Paradise Estate,* an innovative radio soap opera which was written by local schoolchildren and won a Sony Award.

Introducing realistic television training - for both actors and technicians - was more difficult and more costly. Links had already been established with both the BBC and HTV, for students to visit and observe their working studios and sometimes to join in, playing bit-parts, in crowd scenes or as stand-ins. As it became clear that TV would increasingly be actors' main source of income, they really needed hands-on experience at the School. Money to provide professional standard U-matic equipment, the first camera, a desk VTR, a portable VTR (for location work) and a professional standard editing suite was raised by a spectacular production of *Joseph and the Amazing Technicolor Dreamcoat* at the 2,000-seat Bristol Hippodrome in the spring of 1981. Classes and work-experience were introduced for actors and technicians in single camera location work with experienced freelance directors - among them Romey Allison, Jeff Dowson and Colin Godman - and, mainly thanks to the generosity of ex-students, useful additions were gradually made to the stock of equipment.

What the School clearly needed was a television studio where students could practise the techniques involved in programmes like situation comedy, in which many BOVTS-trained actors became familiar faces on TV: Stephanie Cole as Diana in *Waiting for God;* Annette Crosbie as Mrs Victor Meldrew in *One Foot in the Grave;* Peter Denyer in *Please Sir!*; Norman Eshley in *George and Mildred;* Pippa Haywood as Mrs Brittas in *The Brittas Empire;* Ian Lavender as Private Pike in *Dad's Army;* Gavin Richards as the Italian general in *'Allo 'Allo;* Norman Rossington in *The Army Game;* and Patricia Routledge as Hyacinth Bucket in *Keeping Up Appearances.*

Though HTV were helpful and generous in allowing students into their studios when they could be slotted into busy schedules, the only long term solution was obviously for the School to have its own fully-equipped television studio, which was eventually achieved with the active support of BOV Governor John Spielman. Careful budgeting of resources and generous contributions from hundreds of BOVTS graduates gradually built up a fund of £130,000 towards this project, on which work began in the autumn of 1985.

In 1987, the new building - designed by local architects John Collins and Michael Axford, and known at first as the 'VRS' (Video Rehearsal Studio) - replaced a row of damp and musty garages adjacent to the 'NRS' (New Rehearsal Studio) with a television studio and control rooms, plus an urgently needed scenery workshop below. But before it was possible to fund all the new equipment that was part of the plan, more urgent financial problems emerged, threatening the School's very existence.

Since becoming an independent organisation in 1963, the Bristol Old Vic Trust had managed to keep both the Company and the School financially solvent for over twenty-three years in spite of the increasing difficulties faced by regional theatres. In 1986, however, a change of Artistic Director and a complete change of policy precipitated a sudden and severe drop in box-office income and this, coupled with the universal problem of diminishing subsidies, swiftly put the Company in the red. Radical changes to the BOV Board of Governors and the appointment of another Artistic Director in 1987, with yet further changes of policy, did nothing to nip this problem in the bud and, in only two and a half years, the Bristol Old Vic's deficit had risen to £610,000.

As an Associate Director of the Company, which was looking for ways to keep the doors of the Theatre Royal open and the wages paid, Chris Denys found himself involved in an appeal to the Trust's Bankers for a substantial increase in the BOV's overdraft, for which the BOV Trust, being tenants in the Theatre Royal, had only one realisable capital asset to offer as security - the School.

By 1989, it was obvious that the Company could not hope to trade its way back to solvency. In May, the Principal wrote to the Governors summarising the situation and suggesting 'that a new Trust should be set up, to be known, perhaps, as the Bristol Old Vic Theatre School Trust, and that this new Trust purchases the School premises from the Bristol Old Vic Trust for a substantial capital sum to be negotiated ... The immediate advantage to the Company would be the opportunity to make an unencumbered "fresh start" ... From the School's point of view, the only (though substantial) advantage would be the peace of mind and security of being in control of its own future'.

The Governors were understandably reluctant to separate two operations which had worked so successfully side by side since 1946 but Mark Everett, who was then Executive Director of the Company, foresaw a rapidly worsening situation in which 'the Trust would have to consider a commercial disposal of the School to developers'. In June the decision was taken and the Principal was authorised to put his proposal into effect. At that time, the deficit was thought to be £530,000 and, while the School could scrape together the odd £30,000 and, by belt-tightening, take on a mortgage of £300,000, it could not possibly take on the additional debt of £200,000 all in one bite. Help was needed.

Bristol City Council was sympathetic and Walter Miller, then City Treasurer and Acting Chief Executive, gave invaluable help and advice, but it was impossible at that time for the City to offer any financial support. However, David Liddle, Avon's Director of Community Leisure, and David Morgan, the County Treasurer, took a very positive approach, as did the Avon Councillors and, with all-party backing, Avon County Council made a loan to the new Bristol Old Vic Theatre School, Ltd. of £200,000, to be interest-free until 2005.

David Simpson, of Bristol solicitors Trump & Partners, saw the new Company through its formation and registration with the Charity Commissioners and subsequently became Company Secretary. Derek Clark, then Director of Programmes for HTV and a Governor of the Bristol Old Vic Trust, became the first Chairman. Together with Derek Woodcock, then Area Director for the BBC, and Tim Thom, Senior Partner with accountants Price Waterhouse, they formed the Council of Management, which has since been joined by Chartered

Surveyor Don Walker, who has a particular interest in the School's buildings; independent television producer Tamasin Day-Lewis; and Chartered Surveyor Ian Hoddell, chosen for his wide business and professional experience. Mick Escott returned to Bristol in 1989 as the newly-independent School's first Bursar, though along with other staff of the School, which has a very small administration, his work is much broader than the title implies, with involvement in areas ranging from marketing to photography. He had previously been Administration/Finance Manager of the BOV Company (where his responsibilities included the School's finances) from 1983 to 1988, leaving to join commercial producer Bill Kenwright in London as Finance Director.

As the proposed deal involved one registered charity purchasing from another, in order to satisfy the Charity Commissioners, the 'substantial capital sum' which the School paid to secure its independence had to match the Bristol Old Vic Trust's deficit so that the Company could become technically solvent again and be able to continue trading. As the months passed, a further £50,000 was identified in September (which the School agreed to pay off in 2005) and yet another £30,000 in December, which the School must repay in 2010.

While relieved to be in charge of its own financial future, the Theatre School had taken on such large debts that it could not countenance any more expenditure on equipment. It was thanks to £50,000 from the Foundation for Sport and the Arts that the television studio was eventually equipped as a multi-camera facility, using the Betacam system and with its own editing suite, leaving the U-matic systems to operate independently - and often simultaneously - on location and in a separate audio-visual suite. A digital sound-editing system was added in 1994-95, with plans to add a digital video-editing suite, ensuring that graduates of the Stage Management and Technical course (many of whom have become editors) leave with hands-on experience of new techniques.

Chris Denys takes great care to see his School leavers onto the first rung of the employment ladder. Nat Brenner had never found it necessary to set up an organised system of preparing students to launch themselves into the profession, which by the 1960s and 1970s had an established network of potential employers who had been involved with the Bristol Old Vic Company or Theatre School at some point in their career. Everyone who left the School in the 1950s, 1960s and 1970s could confidently expect to get a job, and with it the all-important Equity card that was essential to get work in the profession (for stage managers as well as actors) until the 1990 Employment Act ended the closed shop. But by 1980, there was already a worrying decline in the number of jobs available for actors in theatre, and London agents, managers and directors had become reluctant to spend the time and money on travelling to Bristol to see the final year shows. So Chris Denys introduced a special London showcase of personally-tailored performances by final year students to an invited audience of over four hundred potential employers and agents, giving new performers a list of contacts on which to build in the future.

'Chris teaches you to market yourself as an adviser would anyone setting up their own business, and that's invaluable in the present market-orientated world,' says a recent School leaver. 'Acting is now so much about image - Who are you? What is it about yourself that you're selling? It's not about turning out rep actors who can do everything any more.'

The methods are simple, businesslike and effective. All the students are helped to prepare a well-presented CV, advised how to write letters offering themselves for work, and given all the names and addresses that could help them. In the final year, actors have practice auditions with over two dozen visiting theatre directors and casting directors, sessions with agents, and advice on self-promotion, Equity and life-support systems: 'In your final year you meet lots of professional people who might well give you a job, which breaks down the fear of the unknown and gives you more confidence, because you see the employers as people and get a realistic idea of what they're looking for.' Towards the end of their course, stage managers, technicians, costumiers and designers have practice interviews with production managers and other potential employers from all over the country, having already made some personal contacts through work experience placements.

Whereas Nat Brenner disapproved of the sort of prizes and awards given by other drama schools where, according to one wit, 'you could even get a prize for not getting a prize',

Chris Denys has no objection to awards which offer much-needed cash for a selected few, and several new annual prizes have been established. Since 1980, the student(s) who 'gained most benefit from a non-Acting course' have received the Charles Landstone Award, commemorating the BOV Company's first General Manager. Each year since 1985, local estate agents Chesterton (formerly Lalonde Brothers and Parham) have presented a cash award and trophy to two Acting students, one male, one female, who are usually invited to work with the BOV Company soon after leaving the School. Since 1994, the Bristol Old Vic Theatre Club has made an Award, in tribute to its late Chairman Dennis Cartledge, for the student who 'has contributed most to the life of the School beyond coursework'. And there's a special annual award for comedy acting in memory of 1978 graduate Peter Akerman, whose promising career was cut short by a brain tumour in 1984.

The Theatre School has remained closely involved with the Bristol Old Vic Company, offering both Technical and Acting students regular contact with a real professional environment. When Chris Denys became Principal of the School, John David, who had also been an Associate Director under Val May in the 1960s, became Artistic Director of the Company, presiding over the last few years when the Bristol Old Vic functioned as a more-or-less traditional repertory before the commercial pressures created by Thatcherism made it increasingly difficult for actors to commit themselves to low-paid seasons in regional theatres for months at a time.

When Andrew Hay became Artistic Director of the BOV Company in 1991, he encouraged a much closer working relationship between the Company and the Theatre School than the previous two Artistic Directors, Leon Rubin and Paul Unwin: 'I want students down here to get a taste of working life and the theatre as much as possible. It makes sense - it's all to do with passing on our skills to younger people who will pass them on in the future, that's how theatre has always worked. Not just for the actors but for the Technical students - giving them more time in the Studio so that they don't just rush in and get their show up, they've got a whole week when their lessons can take place in a working studio.'

By the time the second year Technical students staff the

School's productions in the Theatre Royal, New Vic Studio, and Basement, they are already familiar with the BOV Company's technical equipment because some of their first year projects involve planning lighting or sound for the King Street performance spaces. Andrew Hay has also given chances to act in professional BOV Company productions to students in their final year at the Theatre School, notably Jessica Lloyd and Brian McGovern, who played the leads in Brian Friel's *Lovers (Winners)* in the Studio, and Tim Stedman, who joined BOVTS-trained Guy Lankester, Barbara Wilshere and Mark Delaney in *Flare Path* at the Theatre Royal and on tour.

Andrew Hay's Bristol Old Vic Company casts have very often featured Theatre School graduates, most noticeably in his autumn 1994 production of *Twelfth Night,* with seven BOVTS-trained actors, five from the class of 1994 (including Chesterton-winners Guy Lankester and Anna Rose as Orsino and Olivia) and two with many years' experience, Richard Frost as Malvolio and Jill Brassington as Maria. At that time, three more BOVTS graduates had regular roles behind the scenes: Lorraine Laybourne as Deputy Chief Electrician; Barbara Edwards as Wardrobe Assistant; and actor-turned-solicitor Leslie Perrin as Company Secretary. Two more later joined the permanent staff, Darren Portch as a scene painter and Julie Gilliam as a prop maker. Despite the problems of the 1980s, the relationship between the Company and the School has never been better or more constructive than it is in their fiftieth anniversary year.

The School's financial commitments have not prevented a much-needed bit of further building. Since the 1950s, Movement classes had been held in a basement studio where dancers doing lifts or leaps had to take care not to hit the low ceiling. And only in the 'NRS' could a sword be swung indoors without taking out all the light fittings!

For years, the School had unsuccessfully sought planning permission to build a new dance and movement studio on the corner of Pembroke and Downfield Roads. In 1993, surveyor Don Walker's initiative, expertise and persistence finally saw the permission granted. Local architects George Ferguson and John Weir designed the £200,000 studio: 'Funding for this project,' explains Chris Denys, 'was kickstarted by a generous donation from the Mackintosh Foundation, supplemented - as ever - with welcome contributions from ex-students, and several years of careful husbandry of the School's resources.'

Between graduation day in July 1995 and the start of the autumn term in September, the whole building was completed and ready for use. As part of the fiftieth anniversary celebrations, the new building was officially named The Slade/Reynolds Studio, commemorating the writers of *Salad Days,* and several other Downside Road rooms were re-named in honour of important people in the School's development: Acting Studio One as The Duncan Ross Studio; the 'NRS' as The Nat Brenner Studio; the 'VRS' as The John Spielman Television Studio; and Acting Studio Three as The Rudi Shelly Studio.

8. Where do the students come from?

'We were from everywhere,' writes Shane Connaughton, who has acted in rep, with small touring companies and at the National Theatre, as well as being co-writer of the Oscar-nominated film *My Left Foot,* which won Daniel Day-Lewis a 1989 Oscar as Christy Brown. 'I grew up in rural Ireland and London's East End, and went to the Theatre School on an LCC scholarship. I shared a room with Gavin Richards. He had directed a production of *Waiting for Godot* at his school before he came to Bristol - at the age of 15. While at Bristol, we put on the first production of *Saved* by Edward Bond outside the Royal Court. We did it in the University Studio and Bond came to see it. Later I shared a flat with Chris Cazenove who had been to Eton and lived to tell the tale. His father was an old Major in the Guards and did not like Chris acting and thought my 6'1" height a complete waste on the stage when it should have been on a barrack square. John Howell lived in the same house. He had been in the RAF and walked out of a crashed plane alive and into the BOVTS. Rohan McCullough had been to Benenden with princess somebody or other. Sylvia Brayshay was from working class Leeds. Niki Jenkins was from Bath. Barry Startz was from America ... He and our judo teacher George Brandt fought at every judo lesson. Barry had been in the American Army. It was a battle every Saturday morning between the two of them. I remember George had Barry down on the mat, but Barry wouldn't let George's leg go. It went on for hours. The rest of us were pleased. It meant we didn't have to contend with George's well-educated muscles. Philip Weston was another student. He had L written on his left ballet pump and R on his right. I think he was unsure which was which ... Richard Glynne Lewis from Weston-super-Mare always laughed at me in John Oxley's singing lesson. He was from a Welsh family and was a grand warbler. I wasn't. But now when I sing Handel's *L'allegro,* I'm always in that room, looking out at the blossoming cherry tree and thinking of Richard, alas, untimely dead ... I remember Elizabeth from Nigeria. When she brought her African rhythms and movements to bear on the English classics it was marvellous to behold. Eric Maes from Belgium, John Bell from Australia. We were young. We were in love with the work, with life, with each other. Jesus. What more could you want?'

Students of every size, shape, race, nationality, age and social class have trained at the Bristol Old Vic Theatre School. The only thing they all have in common is an unstoppable desire to work professionally as actors and technicians. The passion for theatre - many call it 'getting the bug' - often takes hold very early in life: childhood games inspired Peter Baldwin, who published a book about *Toy Theatres of the World* in 1992; dozens of BOVTS-trained actors said that being taken to see *Peter Pan* when very young was a lasting inspiration; lots were tots under seven when they started putting on shows for their families. Quite a few enjoyed working with youth groups and amateur companies before deciding that for them their hobby was a way of life. Roy Skelton and Robert Lang had both toured with the National Association of Boys Clubs' Travelling Theatre, and many more Bristol students have been actors and techies with the National Youth Theatre.

Locally, Norman Eshley was a leading light of Bristol Youth Theatre, and Milton Johns joined nearly every amateur drama group in Bristol, appearing in more than thirty-five productions in less than five years: 'It was my equivalent of weekly rep,' he smiles. 'One memorable week I was in one play from Monday to Wednesday, then in another play on the other side of town on Thursday, Friday and Saturday.' Amanda Villamayor (first winner of the Julian Slade scholarship for a musically talented student) followed her mother into Bristol Musical Comedy Club and performed with several of Bristol's amateur groups before training at the Theatre School.

Internationally, BOVTS has long established links all over the world. In the years after the war there were usually a few students from the colonies, and in the *Bristol Evening World* of 27 September 1955, the School was described as 'a little United Nations' because about a quarter of the students were from outside the UK, bringing some fascinating characters to

Bristol for a variety of personal reasons. Among them were Rashid Karapiet from Pakistan; Dan Kedar and Ard Feder from Israel; and, from America, Victor Shargai and '24-year-old Jerry Silberman' - later known as Gene Wilder.

George Roman escaped to the West after the Hungarian uprising of 1956, arriving in Bristol via Austrian and English refugee camps: 'In autumn 1957,' he recalls, 'I found myself at the Theatre School in a class with English, Canadian, American, Norwegian and New Zealand students, and, to my amazement, a fellow Hungarian, Sandor Elès; all studying to become actors.'

In the early 1960s, New Zealander Gabriel Prendergast had to train 'overseas' to acquire professional status as a 'producer', and BOVTS was one of the few Schools offering such a course. Several Americans decided to train in England - and in Bristol - because they wanted a technically focused, not emotionally based, training: 'We heard that in England there was a lot of emphasis on the voice and the body, and something called "technique", whereas in New York we're always getting into ourselves, and everything is the Method, going back to Brando, and hailing to Robert de Niro and Al Pacino,' explains Joshua Feinstein. 'The things that De Niro and Pacino do are things that, being a New Yorker and being that type of intense person, I already have inside of me. Well how do I get it out? How do I get it across? I figured the best place to find out was here.'

For some foreign students there was an element of culture shock in their experience of England and the English. American Herb Greer remembers his first Bristol landlady asking him when he would like his bath, and when he suggested 'at night, after the show,' explaining that the price of his Bristol digs included only one bath a week, and she didn't mean what time, but which day. Though British himself, Bristol-trained Bernard Behrens based himself in Canada, where he paved the way for a series of students to cross the Atlantic from Winnipeg to BOVTS. Among them were Evelyne Anderson, Pat Armstrong, Grant Cowan and Edward Evanko, some of whom found Bristol's rain as memorable as the training.

Jack Klaff also shivers to recall the weather - 'I had never experienced cold like that!' but was most affected in the 1970s by the comparative intellectual and artistic freedom:

'There were a number of films and works of literature that were denied to us in South Africa, so that was a very big thing for me. And it was very strange, coming from South Africa at that time of repression and violence, to go to the Blackboy Café on Whiteladies Road.'

Veronica Needa had worked as a stage manager with Chung Ying Theatre in Hong Kong before coming to BOVTS in the early 1980s: 'Although I look quite European in appearance,' she says, 'I am one half Oriental and feel very Chinese inside. It appeared I was behaving in a very un-English way and people found me unsettling without knowing why. I openly worked quite earnestly on everything (a very Hong Kong attribute). It seemed that no-one wanted to go into the front row in the Dance classes (this silly "not wanting to show you're keen" thing) and so I must have trod on toes, so to speak, because I did go into the front row and I was naively keen!'

Many would-be actors, directors and designers come to BOVTS from theatre studies or performing arts courses at further education colleges. Some already have degrees, including a steady intake of students from Bristol University's Drama Department, among them Simon Beresford, Jill Brassington, Allan Corduner, Greg Doran, Alan Dossor, Vincent Franklin, Pippa Haywood, Jane Howell, Eve Karpf, Vivienne McKee, Tim Pigott-Smith, Tim Preece and Marion Reed.

'Acting doesn't require an academic background, it uses a different kind of intelligence, it's an emotionally as well as intellectually analytical approach,' explains Chris Denys, who is determined to resist the minefield of drama school degree courses. 'I personally think it's impossible to study for a drama degree and train to be an actor at the same time, because they're two entirely different approaches to what may look superficially like the same task. Writing an essay about Hamlet is quite another thing from playing the part for three hours at a time, eight performances a week for a month. And drama training is much more akin to dance training than it is to studying plays as if they were literature. It's about teaching people the skills of the craft of acting, not about abstract ideas.'

Those who come to the Theatre School from university have to adjust to a completely different approach to learning. It's not just about the contrasts between 'the drama' and 'the theatre', it's also about basic attitudes towards work: 'There was a group of us who were dubbed "the Clifton Four". We were told that we had a "university attitude" and that wasn't needed, and we were to throw that all away and immerse ourselves in the Theatre School way of working,' recalls Anthony Venditti. 'For the first term and a half I found it quite difficult because at university it's very laid back and you might stroll in for a lecture in the morning, then have one seminar in the afternoon. But at Bristol you had to be there at 8.45 for your warm ups and stay there all day working. I didn't like it at the time, but it was good discipline.'

For some, theatre is already in the family; several well-known names among acting families have turned up in the lists of BOVTS students: 'Our father tried to stop both of us from going into the business,' says Marc Sinden, son of Donald and brother of Jeremy. 'He is one of the point five per cent of this ridiculous profession that works consistently. I remember another actor coming to my parents' house and telling me "You've got to understand that I'm the other side of the business - your father is a success, but I've worked twice in the last four years. That is the reality".' Polly Pleasence was also advised against becoming an actress, 'but when I got into Bristol,' she says, 'my dad was thrilled and he really encouraged me'. Acting families often advise their children to have something to fall back on: Helena Michell took a secretarial course before training as an actress; and both Lucy Briers and Katy Secombe took university degrees before coming to Bristol.

There are frequently family connections within the School. Sophie Thompson chose Bristol because her mother, Phyllida Law, had trained at BOVTS, her father Eric Thompson - best known for *The Magic Roundabout* - was a member of the BOV Company, and her parents had been married at 'the actors' church', St George's, Brandon Hill, one morning before a matinée of *A Midsummer Night's Dream* at the Theatre Royal. Samantha and Abigail Bond - daughters of television producer Pat Sandys, who played Abigail in the British premiere production of *The Crucible* at Bristol Old Vic in 1954 and Philip Bond, who played in BOV's *Christmas in King Street* and is best known for *The Onedin Line* - both trained at Bristol, as did Sean and Dariel Pertwee, sisters Katie and Susan Tordoff, and actor

Francis Matthews' sons, Paul Rattigan and Damien Matthews. Sonia Fraser, who was an Acting student at BOVTS in the 1950s and has returned since the late 1980s as a guest director and teacher, encouraged her son Tristian Bickerton to train at Bristol: 'If I was rehearsing or working in the theatre and Tristian came by, I could see that it had the magic for him that it had for me, and I thought "Oh my God he's going to be an actor!" I was delighted when he went in on the technical side, which to me meant more security and a much better life than I knew actors had.'

Several children from theatrical families, not wanting to work as performers, have trained at BOVTS for other roles: Stephanie Cole's daughter Emma Battcock and Jean Boht's daughter Jessie Davis trained as stage managers; Siobhan O'Casey, daughter of playwright Sean, was a Design student; and James Barlow, son of Thelma Barlow (*Coronation Street*'s Mavis Riley, and a former member of the BOV Company) and Graham Barlow (who was for many years BOV's Resident Designer) spent a year at BOVTS on a Director's Attachment.

The proportion of women to men at the Theatre School has changed significantly. Just after the war, there were many more women than men, and most of the male students were ex-servicemen, recently 'de-mobbed' from the wartime armed forces. In the 1950s and 1960s, the numbers of men and women student actors were fairly even, but since the 1970s there have been significantly fewer places for women, reflecting the availability of jobs in the working world: in the classical theatre, there are eight times as many roles for men as for women. There were very few women stage managers in the professional theatre right up to the mid-1970s, but by the 1990s, women applying to train as stage managers at BOVTS outnumbered men by three to one - and only one man has ever taken the Wardrobe course.

Two years' compulsory National Service for all young men continued until December 1960, making the average age of male students generally higher - between twenty-one and twenty-four (depending on whether they'd also been to university) - than the girls, who were often only seventeen or eighteen. Peter Birrel made a virtue out of a necessity: he auditioned and secured his BOVTS place before doing his National Service, then 'honed my microphone technique babbling jargon to pilots from Air Traffic Control'.

It's undoubtedly easier to make a start in such a physically demanding and financially insecure profession as acting when you're young: it's easier to get fit and stay fit; and you can more readily afford to take a chance before the expenses of adult life set in. The first BOVTS prospectus simply required applicants to be 'over fifteen', compared with the London Old Vic Theatre School's age limits of seventeen to twenty-three for trainee actors in the 1940s. By 1954, BOVTS advertised an age range between sixteen and twenty-seven, though Duncan Ross was in the vanguard of accepting mature students: Michael Lynch recalls starting his course at the grand old age of thirty-one, in a group of very young students including sixteen-year-olds Stephanie Cole and Patricia Brake. Since the early 1980s, the age range for applicants has stayed at eighteen to thirty, and although anyone younger than eighteen would be recommended to go away and get some experience of life before re-applying, there is always room for the over-thirties if they have the right talent and personality to do the job - and the money to pay for the training. In recent years, Chris Denys has accepted lawyers and bankers in their forties, and a schools' inspector in his fifties, all of whom went on to make a living as actors.

People have given up an astonishing variety of other careers and secure jobs to try their luck and their talent as actors: 'You name it - we've had 'em,' smiles Elwyn Johnson, 'doctors, marketing men, civil servants, maths teachers, science teachers - drama teachers! - welders, farmers, restaurant managers, journalists, computer programmers...'

Faced, at the age of forty-two, with two choices - either 'to be a Labour MP or go to drama school' - David Frederickson, former Sheffield City Councillor and Chair of the Planning Committee, trained at BOVTS and became a professional actor. Christopher Mellows had worked in banking for twenty-seven years, and was forty-five when he took voluntary redundancy and came to BOVTS for a change of career: 'I'd always done a lot of amateur theatre, and I came here hoping they could teach an old dog new tricks! I wanted to confirm for myself that I knew how to act.' And he did, leaving in the summer of 1995 for a fifteen-week tour of *The Darling Buds of May.*

Before auditioning at BOVTS in the late 1960s, Tim

Barlow had been in the army for fifteen years and was quite deaf from the effects of close-range gunfire. Nevertheless, Nat Brenner and John Oxley believed he was trainable, and he has made his living mainly as an actor for over twenty years: 'There's no problem that comes up while working that you can't get over, absolutely none. On stage, if there's a cue I can't hear, they get someone to do something visual - and in comedy it's amazing how it makes all the actors much more physical than they would have been. I can lip-read monitor screens in television studios. The main problem is getting the job in the first place. If a director is seeing a lot of actors, and he's confronted with one who can't hear him first time, he's often not interested. It's been much better since I worked with Théâtre de Complicité - when they first started they were a mime company!'

It's not unusual for performers to have had professional experience as actors, dancers or comedians before taking a course at BOVTS. Some found it difficult to get very far without the prestige of an accredited drama school on their CV. For those who had achieved some success with natural talent, the Theatre School could provide the depth and range of skills for which they'd come to feel a need: 'After five years, I had reached a point where I was being challenged with parts in which I couldn't get by purely on instinct,' says John Sharian, who later played the leading role in Andrew Hay's BOV production of O'Neill's *The Hairy Ape*.

'I found myself coming off stage every night really frustrated, knowing what I wanted to do but not knowing how to do it,' admits Aled Jones, who became a household name as a boy soprano, then studied for three years at the Royal Academy of Music as a singer before being faced with two choices: 'You can either learn by your mistakes - just get an agent and go out there and do it; or you can go to theatre school.' He chose to train at BOVTS, and 'now I'm a lot more aware of what I'm doing on stage, whereas before I just did it.'

'I particularly wanted not to limit myself,' says Tony Howes, who had played the Artful Dodger in *Oliver!* before he went to BOVTS. 'I could have quite easily gone from the National Youth Theatre to playing Cockney geezers on television, and just done the one thing, but training at the

Theatre School means I have a versatile career now, from whacky children's television to Shakespeare with the Oxford Stage Company and musicals in the West End.' After BOVTS, Tony's first job was in the original West End musical of *Adrian Mole,* and he returned to Bristol in 1995 co-starring with Paul Nicholas as comic sidekick Cosmo in *Singin' In The Rain* at the Hippodrome: 'I'm what Tommy Steele calls "a triple threat" - someone who can sing and dance and act.'

9. Why theatre school? Why Bristol?

In the 1940s, the London and Bristol Old Vic Theatre Schools were unusual in their direct link with professional producing companies, offering structured training 'on the job' rather than only the training or mainly the job. Long after the first British drama school - the London Academy of Music and Dramatic Art (LAMDA) - had been founded in 1861, most actors expected to learn their trade by trial and error with an established provincial company. Though enthusiasm and raw talent may get you started, many professional actors say that a thorough grounding in technique is essential to keep them going. It's one thing to walk and talk or sing and dance your way through a part once, twice - even for a week. But quite another to do it six nights a week and two matinées for months on end. Actors need to understand, strengthen, and then regularly exercise their bodies and their voices - the tools of their trade.

More training schools were set up at the turn of the twentieth century, notably the Royal Academy of Dramatic Art (RADA) in 1904, and the Central School of Speech and Drama in 1906, followed by the forerunners of today's Arts Educational Schools in 1919 and 1922, Webber Douglas in 1926, and Birmingham School of Speech and Drama in 1936. The optimistic atmosphere in Britain immediately after the 1939-45 war encouraged the foundation of several new drama schools, notably the Welsh College of Music and Drama in 1946, and Rose Bruford College of Speech and Drama in 1950 as well as the Old Vic's new Theatre Schools in London and Bristol. A second flowering in the early 1960s produced East 15 (1961), Drama Centre (1962), the Guildford School of Acting (1964) and Mountview, which has operated a School since 1969 after starting out as a producing company in 1945. All of these, including the Bristol Old Vic Theatre School, are members of the Conference of Drama Schools, the professional association set up in 1969 to monitor standards and represent the interests of both the students and the institutions.

'One key thing about BOVTS was that it was in Bristol rather than in London,' says Rob Edwards. 'The big gain was that as a student actor you were allowed to learn, practise, and *fail* (a crucial part of any learning process) out of the spotlight as it were, whereas actors from London schools often complain that they were conscious of being judged by important people in the business from day one.'

The major advantage of the BOV Theatre School has always been its close association with the BOV Company - and, until 1963, the London Old Vic too. In its early years, when the School was based across the road from the stage door, the students felt very much like apprentices, learning their trade not only in formal classes but also from working alongside the professional actors. They knew that they were on the bottom rung of a meritocracy: at the Old Vic, you could go in as a spear carrier and end up playing leading roles.

The head of the BOV Theatre School has always been an Associate Director of the Company, and all but one (Richard Ainley) worked at the Theatre Royal as either director or performer - Edward Stanley did both. Between 1992 and 1995 Chris Denys has co-written and directed four annual pantomimes for the Bristol Old Vic Company in the Theatre Royal, and in the summer of 1996 was already preparing a fifth, with co-writer Chris Harris (a regular guest director/teacher at BOVTS) as the regular Dame.

Graduate productions have always been presented on the Bristol Old Vic's professional stages: 'It's a great feeling to come in through the stage door, and do your rehearsal in the BOV Rehearsal Room while there are other shows going on - it really does feel like you're *There!*'

Working with the Company was very much a part of the training in the late 1940s and 1950s when Equity regularly allowed six students from the School - four actors and two backstage - to take part in each professional production. Some worked more than others: young Norman Rossington proved himself a useful character actor for forty-odd weeks on seven productions, with casts including Dorothy Tutin, Patrick McGoohan, and 'the two Donalds - Sinden and Pleasence. Where I really learnt was in the Theatre Royal, doing the job with this marvellous Company. There's no substitute for that. It worked out very well: I used to pop over from across the road to rehearsals, and back to the School for classes.'

It didn't work out quite so well for fellow-student Susan Dowdall, when she played Maria in *The School for Scandal*, directed by Edward Stanley and starring Donald Pleasence and John Neville: 'While I was in the wings after the screen scene, I accidentally brushed my skirt against the fire extinguisher, and it went off, very noisy and squirting everywhere. I still have this vision of John Neville, who was waiting to go on, picking it up and disappearing through the exit door!'

After the School moved up to Clifton in 1955, students were often back down in King Street helping backstage, and sometimes playing small parts. Robert Lang had already appeared in four professional productions before being taken straight into the BOV Company on leaving the School. Stephanie Cole remembers working as a dresser during her second term in 1959, and making her professional debut on the Theatre Royal stage during her second year - as a ninety-year-old woman in *The Woodcarver,* when she was herself not yet nineteen! Peter Layton, founder and Executive Director of the Drama Studio in London's Ealing, was one of several BOVTS students who appeared as teenage rebels in *The Pier* with Peter O'Toole.

Each year, a chosen few School-leavers were offered their first job with the Company. Among the actors who began successful careers in this way are Patrick Blackwell, Mark Buffery, Simon Cadell, Stephanie Cole, Jeremy Child, Kenneth Cope, Daniel Day-Lewis, Susan Engel, Norman Eshley, Nicholas Farrell, Ian Gelder, Carole Hayman, Pippa Haywood, Pat Heywood, Jeremy Irons, Milton Johns, Janet Key, Ingrid Lacey, Mark Lambert, Jane Lapotaire, Phyllida Law, Caroline Loncq, Tim Pigott-Smith, Louise Plowright, Pete Postlethwaite, Paul Rattigan, Amanda Redman, David Roper, Norman Rossington, Adrian Scarborough, Roy Skelton, Patrick Stewart, John Telfer, Sophie Thompson, Ann Way and John Webb.

'When I came out of drama school I felt that there wasn't any part I couldn't play brilliantly,' recalls Jeremy Child. 'I was thrilled to be taken on by the Bristol Old Vic, and to see God - as Val May was known. I remember arriving a week before the season started to be met by the Stage Manager, who said "Get that bucket, get that brush and get painting those dressing rooms". So I spent the first week of my professional career painting the dressing rooms at Bristol Old Vic, which was very thrilling....... But then we started rehearsals for a musical called *Lock Up Your Daughters,* which was wonderful. I had to do everything: get the props; be in it; sweep the stage; take tea to the actors. I was a general dogsbody, but it was marvellous because that was where I wanted to be.'

Amanda Redman was asked to join the Company in her last term at the School, and stayed for a year at an exciting time when Artistic Director Richard Cottrell was putting shows on three stages at once (the Theatre Royal, New Vic, and Little Theatre) and when Adrian Noble, who went on to run the RSC, was an Assistant Director. Louise Plowright's first season included the title role in Willy Russell's two-hander *Educating Rita* in the New Vic, and a tour of local pubs with a studio production of *Totterdown Tanzi* (a Bristolised *Trafford*) as Platinum Sue: 'I was incredibly lucky,' she says. 'Not many actors leave drama school and straightaway play leading roles in a good rep like the Bristol Old Vic. And being in rep - rehearsing during the day and doing another play at night - was like another year's training.'

The Company has also offered many a first job to the School's backstage trainees. In the 1950s, Jane Angles and Bob Harris worked together at the Theatre Royal as two of the first ever Technical students and both stayed on: he as an ASM; she as Assistant Wardrobe Mistress. In the 1990s, Clare England's first job was four years as a BOV Company Technician, and for Ashley Bale it was four weeks as Acting Chief Electrician for the Bristol Old Vic.

Of the many BOVTS graduates who found first jobs elsewhere and later returned to work with the BOV Company, undoubtedly the most popular has been June Barrie, who became a regular every season for ten years between 1972 and 1983 (including playing Lilian Baylis in Chris Denys' 1974 centenary production) and has also frequently been heard in BBC radio drama. Others include Roger Bizley, Samantha Bond, Patricia Brake, Jill Brassington, Susan Colverd, Annette Crosbie, Neil Cunningham, Stephen Dillane, Susan Dowdall,

Julia Ford, Richard Frost, Stephen Gray, Michael Hadley, Ingrid Hafner, Daniel Hill, Alex Jennings, Timothy Kightley, Jack Klaff, Robert Lang, Barbara Leigh-Hunt, Sara Markland, Sally Mates, John McEnery, Dariel Pertwee, Miranda Richardson, Patricia Routledge, Greta Scacchi, Maggie Steed, and Kit Thacker.

But enough of this name-dropping! None of the hundreds of ex-students who helped with the research for this book went to Bristol because of the famous people who trained there. On the contrary: most of them, like Timothy Bentinck, chose BOVTS because 'it had a reputation for producing working actors as opposed to stars'. This attitude has long been a deliberate part of the School's policy. Duncan Ross's students remember being told: 'I am not training the stars of tomorrow, I am preparing the working actors of the next decade.'

Jeremy Irons went straight into the BOV Company from the School, starting by playing walk-ons and leaving playing juvenile leads like Florizel in *The Winter's Tale* and Simon in *Hay Fever:* 'If you wanted to be a star, you would go to RADA,' he explains. 'If you wanted to be an actor and a musician, you went to LAMDA. If you wanted to be an actor and a teacher, you went to Central. And if you wanted to be a new-wave, kitchen-sink sort of actor, you went to East 15, which was pretty new at that time. But Bristol was where you trained to be an all-round repertory actor, a bloke who could play anything, and subsume himself in the part rather than shine as a star.'

10. Auditions - please choose *me*

It's all very well for would-be actors to choose Bristol - but how does the Theatre School choose them? Keeping a close eye on the requirements of the industry for which it is training people, BOVTS is careful to take in only as many students as are reasonably expected to find work when they leave: on average about twenty-six each year, and significantly fewer women.

Student actors usually get places in the same way as stage actors get jobs, by auditions - a gruelling process of doing your party pieces in front of a critical audience who know exactly what they want and that there's plenty more where you came from. Students have to pay to audition, so 'doing the rounds' of applying to several drama schools can be an expensive business. In 1954 the audition fee at BOVTS was 'half a guinea' - the quaint tradition of calculating theatre finances by the guinea (one pound one shilling - now 105 new pence) continued until 1971, when the new decimal currency was introduced. By 1957, the BOVTS audition fee had risen to one guinea, doubling again by 1959 and staying fixed at two guineas until 1972, when it went up to £3.50. In 1996, prospective students paid £20 for a preliminary audition, and another £20 if they were recalled for the next stage of selection. Overseas students sometimes auditioned for a Bristol representative in their own country, but were often accepted on evidence of their past work - plus a cash deposit of a full year's fees.

Most drama schools see applicants at only one audition, which some students have likened to 'a cattle-market', where they did their practised pieces before a quite formal panel, which then asked questions. In the 1940s and 1950s, BOVTS also chose its students from single auditions, but now those who show promise at a preliminary audition with one of the staff are invited to Bristol for a 'Weekend School': 'It was the most thorough of all the drama schools I applied to,' says one student. 'They find out a lot more about you as a person, and your abilities, before they decide to take you'; 'It was an opportunity to work with others, to communicate rather than showing off alone,' says another. 'I felt that any school that took so much time and trouble to see the "real you" had the best chance of spotting your potential and was also likely to be the most discerning in who it chose.'

When Nat Brenner first introduced the Weekend School in 1964, everyone who applied was invited, but that was soon abandoned as impractical because of the large numbers involved. Even so, the staff spend several weekends each year working with prospective students in a process that one described as 'a kind of little activity holiday'. Over the two days, at least six teachers have a chance to assess the would-be actors not only for individual talent, but also for how well they work with other people in the group, and whether they are open to taking advice and learning from constructive criticism. For some students, it's their first real experience of what training as an actor actually involves: 'The Weekend School was a sort of précis of the whole course, a bit of voice, movement and text study with all the teachers,' explains Rena Valeh.

About thirty students arrive in Bristol on a Friday night, each armed with two prepared speeches (one Shakespeare, one modern) and an unaccompanied song, ready to be divided into five groups of six, one of which is thrown in at the deep end to a Movement class with Gail Gordon: 'I remember thinking I could cruise the dance audition because I'd done so much dancing when I was younger but there was no pulling the wool over Gail Gordon's eyes,' says Sara Markland. 'She just said "You can do a deeper plié than that" and I was absolutely knackered by the end of it! But I loved it - I was so challenged by the whole weekend.'

Several students who were less fit at the time remember being hardly able to get out of bed and walk on the Saturday morning after Gail's class on Friday night. And the regime was just as tough with the previous movement teacher: 'She wanted us to rise halfway off the floor and do our speeches, which I could easily do because I was quite fit and my stomach muscles were hard as a board,' recalls John Telfer, who thinks 'it was Nat who got me into the School because when we were doing a crowd scene I was joining in a lot, generally "being a citizen", and he probably thought "Good company man" - one of his familiar sayings.'

Students were often surprised to find that they had to do physical jerks alongside their audition pieces: lying on the floor 'bicycling', or throwing a medicine ball to each other. Dariel Pertwee's group had to say their speeches while skipping, 'but I could only skip double time,' recalls Dariel. 'Rudi thought this was hysterical and taught me to skip slowly.'

'When Rudi had us all on the floor declaiming our Shakespeare piece while doing continuous sit-ups, it nearly killed me but it seemed the most natural thing in the world,' writes Allison Hancock. 'It was as if I'd been living with a different species all my life - like a starling in a flock of geese - and had discovered that there were others like me after all. I felt as if I had come home.'

Another group was asked to do their prepared speech in gobbledegook, and have the other students try to say what they thought the character was like before hearing it again as it was written: 'Very illuminating. You had to instantly transfer all those thoughts and images into a completely bizarre language which you made up on the spot, and you soon discovered whether you'd communicated the point.'

'They were obviously looking for people who could co-operate with others, who could listen to direction, and who had a bit of a go,' writes Brian Austin. 'Rudi would ask you to read from the phone book and then ask why you had done it. The answer "because you asked me" was *nil points!* I remember saying I was a bookie's clerk passing on names of punters.'

Very many students had to apply more than once to get into the Bristol Old Vic Theatre School, demonstrating the single-minded belief in themselves and their career choice that actors really need to succeed. One was so determined to get in that when she was not offered a place the first time, she moved to Bristol, took a job in an office and applied again and again: 'I told them after the second time that I would be back until they let me in and I think tenacity won through. Because there are so few places for women - only four in my year group - it's a hell of boost when you do get one.'

In the early days of BOVTS, auditions were often quite informal. Arriving for his audition at Queen Charlotte Street,

Roy Skelton met Anthony Holland, the Assistant Director. 'He said that he had just started to put fencing into the School programme. I told him that I had fenced for Bomber Command when I was in the forces and he became excited at this and we went across the road and he got the foils out. We had a few hits - and I won! I think that's how I got into the School.' There was another hurdle first, when Mr Skelton was asked if he wanted to do his audition speech privately for the staff or in front of the whole school: 'I was terrified, but felt that if I didn't say "in front of the whole school" I wouldn't stand a chance. I shudder now at the thought that the Shakespeare I chose was Othello's last speech - Oh what it is to be young and unafraid!'

Before applying to BOVTS in 1958, Michael Lynch had already had a 'very painful' audition at RADA, doing a speech from *Othello,* 'extremely nervous and solitary under the eyes of unseen judges in the darkened stalls of the Vanbrugh Theatre. By contrast, 'Bill Ross greeted me personally and we chatted briefly. He led me into one of the large rooms of the School, sat himself down in an attentive but studiously relaxed pose and invited me to show him what I had prepared - a Trofimov speech from *The Cherry Orchard.* He let me finish, and then asked me to start again, but to have in mind a totally different objective. I found myself exploring the variety of colours that come naturally as one changes the effect one tries to have on the listener. It was exciting ... and after about three-quarters of an hour, Bill Ross asked me if I would like to start at the School next term!'

Forty years on, Peter Birrel vividly recalled his audition for Duncan Ross in 'a largish, empty room' where, after he'd done his prepared bits, Ross 'put several items, coins, a pencil, perhaps, in a curving line on the floor. "Start in the far corner," he said. "Come towards the table here, picking up each of these things on your way." Aha, thought I, must be elegant, and - casual as you like - bent knees, not back, to do the retrieving. I expect Bill smiled knowingly to himself: self-conscious twerp, he must have thought.' There was only one more hurdle: asked to name his favourite actor, Mr Birrel prevaricated, wondering what would make the right impression: 'I don't know if I have single favourite,' he hedged, 'I mean, how can you compare Olivier, Gielgud, Humphrey Bogart ....' 'Good,' Mr Ross interrupted, 'I think you'll do.'

There are several tales of people turning up for auditions and mistaking Nat Brenner for a caretaker or handyman: 'I'd seen this old boy in the garden, and I just assumed he was the gardener!' says Philip Childs. 'When I went in to the session with three others, he was sitting there, but no-one introduced him or said who he was. Then when we were asked to read, one of the other auditionees said he was dyslexic, and the other one - trying to score a point - remarked that Susan Hampshire is dyslexic, at which Nat said "Yes, but she's got amazing tits, hasn't she". And I remember thinking, this is no normal teacher!'

Rudi Shelly looks for three qualities in a person who might make a good actor: 'Do you love to play? Do you love to communicate - bodily, vocally and mentally? And do you love good craftsmanship?' Chris Denys looks for people 'who are so intrinsically interesting that others will pay money to look at them'.

After being accepted by the School, many students have had to undergo another gruelling audition in order to persuade their local authority to help pay their way. The specific requirements vary considerably from place to place and year to year, and it's very much a lottery. Quite a number of Bristol students greatly improved their chances of winning by knowing someone on the funding panel personally! Often this would be through a common interest in the theatre, because many authorities would ask local drama advisors or professional actors or directors to help make the selection, though it was not unusual for would-be students to be asked to read poems or speeches to people who had no connection with theatre whatsoever.

'I don't think they realised theatre technicians existed,' says one student, who applied for funding from Kent in the late 1960s. 'They latched onto the fact that I wanted to go to drama school, and insisted that I should audition for them - an excruciating experience for all concerned. As a concession, having pointed out to them that I was not going to act, I was allowed to do only one piece instead of two, and I had to learn a speech of Queen Elizabeth's from a play called *Will Shakespeare*. It was dreadful! Anyway, they gave me a discretionary grant of £30 a term and my father had to continue to support me and pay my fees.' Cambridgeshire in the 1990s actually charged a fee of £80 to consider an application for a grant! Having paid up, one BOVTS student had to prepare a speech, a song and a dance, even though she was also going to train as a stage manager.

Since 1980, an integral part of the training for Bristol's Acting students involves preparing for an audition every three weeks throughout their course: sometimes for the teachers; sometimes in front of other students; sometimes on video so that they can see their own mistakes; and, as they come nearer to leaving, for more than twenty artistic directors, casting directors and agents, who are specially invited to the School for a day. As well as offering useful on-the-spot advice on how to do it better, these visiting professionals have the chance to make a mental note of promising actors they might later like to use - and often do. Neal Foster, actor-manager of the Birmingham Stage Company (the resident company at Birmingham Old Rep), Karl James, Associate Director of the Oxford Stage Company, Sheffield Artistic Director Deborah Paige, and casting director Brian Wheeler all trained as actors at BOVTS and are regularly invited back to audition students.

The format of the practice auditions varies: sometimes it's two speeches and a song; another time one modern, one classical speech and a song; and 'in the first year, the infamous dance audition - one speech, a song, and sixteen bars of self-choreographed dance, which is absolutely hideous. You go in with your little tape, do your speech, then take your outer clothes off and do this ridiculous dance routine in front of everybody! I think it's intended as part of getting over any embarrassment about your body, and for some of us it was probably the most embarrassing moment of our lives!'

The actors are advised to develop a range of audition pieces that will show off different aspects of their character, not to limit themselves to what they find easy or obvious. So students leave with a full repertoire that runs the gamut of their ability: 'By the time I left Bristol I had twenty-seven speeches that I'd done and nine that I could do at the drop of a hat,' says Samantha Bond. 'I'd go to interviews and they'd say "What are you going to do?" and I'd be able to say "What would you like to see?" They might have already seen Rosalind fifteen times that morning, but I could do Phoebe, Hermione, and several more.'

When Patrick Miller auditioned for the RSC, some of the panel arrived late: 'They asked me to do my pieces again, and I asked if I could do two different ones instead - I think that probably helped me to get in.' Patrick, who toured America in 1995 as Shakespeare's Romeo, is well known to Bristol Old Vic audiences as the perennial silly sidekick to pantomime Dame Chris Harris.

When actors become better known in the business - not necessarily well known to the public - they're more likely to be invited to read for specific parts than to do a conventional audition. And going up for a part in a TV advert is a completely different experience: 'You just have to go in, state your name, look one way, look the other way, hit a mark without looking at the floor, and then it's "Next!" from thousands of people who are up for it.'

In television drama, producers tend to use people of the same age, appearance and accent as the character. Gillian Lewis now finds 'I'm too old for mothers, but I don't look old enough for grandmothers. I went up for something not long ago when I was supposed to be the daughter of someone who was eighty-five, and they said "You're fifteen years too young". But actually I was five years too old! These days it's the looks that matter because there are so many people out of work that they can cast exactly the looks they want. I do still work, but I'm in a limbo - five foot five and greying blonde - where there's nothing in commercials at all because one's not an aunt, not a mother, not anything.'

'When I started in rep, I often played characters much older than I was really - with a wig and a false beard,' recalls Roger Bizley. 'Now I am that age and have a real beard, I tend to get cast as a lot of sea captains! It's one of the ways the business has changed - nowadays they cast someone who already looks, sounds or is the character they want rather than expecting you to act it.'

Despite all the changes in the industry, auditions still have their place as the main selection process in the theatre. And every year since 1970, one lucky student at Bristol Old Vic Theatre School has a little extra help with those all-important early auditions - a cash award that can help to kit out a deserving new graduate in smart clothes to impress potential employers. This prize, for an impressive comedy performance, is given in memory of Newton Blick, who was an actor with the Bristol Old Vic Company in the 1950s. Legend has it that Mr Blick was at the theatre in King Street one day when he heard there was a fire at his Park Street digs. He rushed up the hill and dashed into the burning building to rescue his only set of respectable clothes, his 'audition suit'!

11. Who pays for all this?

Very often, the students themselves. Or their families. Over the years various government or LEA (Local Education Authority) grants have been available but always under arbitrarily restricted conditions. A host of charitable trusts and foundations - detailed in publications like the Welfare Association's *Money to Study,* and *The Directory of Grant Making Trusts* - offer funding for theatre school training. Companies of Drapers, Skinners and Fishmongers have been known to support theatre students; others have qualified for help by being the second daughter of a Rear Admiral, for example, or the child of a church Minister.

Official funding for drama training can seem just as bizarre. In the 1940s, government money for educational courses, including drama training, was given to ex-servicemen like David Chivers, but not to state registered nurses like Mary Sedgewick, who worked three night shifts a week at a hospital during her first term to make ends meet. In the 1990s, local authorities' responsibility for funding education obliges them to provide schooling for all children up to their mid-teens, but further education only for some. Subject to a means-tested contribution from better-off parents, studying for degrees automatically qualifies for 'mandatory' awards covering all course fees and some help with living costs. But many of those with the talent and determination to get a place on a vocational course are eligible only for 'discretionary' funding.

Whether or not you got a grant was a hit-and-miss affair that unfairly depended more on geography and politics than on talent: in one of the last years before central government charge-capping took away local government's control over local finance, one of the Yorkshire authorities gave out £13.7 million in discretionary awards for vocational training while, in the same year, Avon County Council gave £440,000. In the three years before Avon - Bristol's own LEA - was dissolved in April 1996, it gave no discretionary awards at all because of fears of overspending.

Two-thirds of the students at Michel Saint-Denis' London Old Vic Theatre School in the late 1940s and early 1950s were on local authority scholarships, and it's likely that this also applied to Bristol at that time. Most Local Education Authorities (then called County Education Committees) in the late 1950s were generous with funds for theatre students. Expansive attitudes towards further education in the 1960s and early 1970s led to the founding of several new universities and drama schools, to which students from less well-off families were encouraged to go by a comparatively generous provision of public funding: the 1965-66 BOVTS prospectus noted that although an offer of a place did not guarantee a grant, 'the chances are that in most cases an award will be made'. Twenty out of twenty-two UK Acting students who applied for funding and joined the School for the course in September 1964 - and in 1965 all twenty-four Acting students - were granted a 'Further Education Award'. Of the Technical students, twelve out of the fifteen on the course in 1964-65 were given grants - and fourteen out of eighteen in 1965-66.

It was after the election of Margaret Thatcher as Conservative Prime Minister in 1979 that the emphasis shifted decisively from 'public expansion' to 'private enterprise' and government attitudes towards education and public spending severely reduced the financial support given for all kinds of training, by such measures as replacing grants with loans, and excluding all students from claiming housing benefit. It wasn't just theatre people who were victimised: clergymen, lawyers, architects, osteopaths and farmers were also dependent on discretionary awards for their vocational training. But those training for the theatre were particularly hard hit, despite the economic reality that show business gradually took over from cars, shipbuilding, iron, steel and even banking as Britain's largest export.

'In 1996 there are over a hundred and thirty Local Education Authorities,' says Chris Denys. 'Some will give discretionary awards for drama training, some want to but can't - they've been charge-capped, they've got derelict schools with no books, and paper sheets on their hospital beds. And some wouldn't give it for drama even if they had it. I find the increasing difficulties over discretionary funding doubly bewildering because "vocational training" - training for actual employment - is what the Government says higher education should be about. Yet it's particularly hard to obtain grants for Stage Management students, even though the employment prospects for our graduates couldn't be better.'

In 1993 only thirty-nine per cent of local authorities provided any money at all for drama students, compared with eighty-three per cent in 1987, and in 1994 one in six LEAs gave no discretionary awards at all. One consequence of this drastic reduction in discretionary funding was for some drama schools to re-fashion their courses to include the kind of academic study that would qualify for a degree, as much for the sake of fitting into the arbitrary mould of the grant system as for any educational benefit. Apart from RADA, LAMDA, Webber Douglas and Bristol, by 1996 all of the previously vocational theatre school members of the Conference of Drama Schools had taken the academic path and become degree courses.

'We regard it as a seductive self-destruct button,' says Chris Denys, who remained determined to offer a purely vocational training at Bristol Old Vic Theatre School. 'The results speak for themselves: far greater numbers of students in training, staff to student ratios much higher than our one to three, loss of the freedom to adapt the curriculum to the changing needs of the profession, a completely contradictory approach to the task - talking about it, reading about it, theorising about it but not *doing* it the way it needs to be done. At the end of the day, a large number of those who have already graduated from these courses and *still* want to act, then apply to us for *vocational* training. By then, of course, what small likelihood there might have been of a discretionary award has been blown away by the fact that they've just spent three years at "university".'

Unlike many other training institutions, The Bristol Old Vic Theatre School is completely unsubsidised, relying on student fees to provide nearly ninety per cent of its income, and on its status as a registered charity to help that income stretch a little further than it otherwise might. A small but significant part of the School's income comes from public productions, and there are also contributions from charitable trusts, business sponsors, ex-students and private individuals, enabling the

School to keep its training facilities up to the 'state of the art' and in line with professional standards and usage. The Bristol Old Vic Theatre Club, founded in July 1946, has long supported the School as well as the Company. For many years the Club has given direct sponsorship to School productions, and in the mid-1990s amended its constitution to include supporting the School's work. It has provided willing helpers on all sorts of occasions and arranged fund-raising events including sponsored walks led by Jane Lapotaire, who has been President of the Theatre Club since 1986. Individual members have generously provided students with accommodation, employment, nourishment, and friendship.

In addition to inviting students to produce plays at its Barn Theatre in Devon, the Dartington Trust showed a generous financial interest in the BOV Theatre School in the 1940s, providing some money for deserving students such as David Chivers and Mary Sedgewick, who shared a small award, and went on to tour the reps as a husband-and-wife team (known as a 'joint'). The first scholarship to study at BOVTS was awarded in the second year of the School's existence by playwright J B Priestley, enabling Arthur Sibley, who had taken evening classes in 1946-47, to become a full-time student for a year. Since 1972, Bristol University Drama graduates who go on to BOVTS for vocational training have benefited from the Rapier Players Scholarship, a small but significant grant from a fund set up by Ronald Russell and Peggy Ann Wood with money remaining after the closure of their independent company, which had presented plays in weekly, then fortnightly, rep at the Little Theatre in Bristol's Colston Street for twenty-eight years between 1935 and 1963.

The Mackintosh Foundation has been generous in its support of the School's core courses, and in its contribution to the building of the new dance studio; and the Foundation for Sport and the Arts not only helped to equip the School's television studio but also, in 1993, gave its first ever individual grant to help a BOVTS Stage Management student with her living costs. The School has attracted sponsorship from a wide selection of benefactors, including the School's Bankers for the West Country Tour, a local brewery for the Stage Management students' welding course and a film production company for the work of the School as a whole.

Charitable funds have been set up as memorials to staff and students who have died: Ian Adley, Peter Akerman, Madeleine Farrell, Jean Healey, Janet Key, and most recently Nat Brenner. Other help has come from private individuals who take a special interest in BOVTS, and from innumerable ex-students, not listed here for fear of their being drowned in a deluge of begging letters. Benefactors include Mrs John Spielman, widow of a former governor of the BOV Trust, and (as Paula Gwyn-Davies) a former Secretary of the School; orchestra manager Bill Occleshaw (who provides musicians for anything from full-scale shows to practice auditions); theatrical agent Michelle Braidman; and the late Peter Crouch. School Chaplain Neville Boundy, a key part of the School's pastoral care arrangements, donated the entire box-office from a performance of his play *Father & Son, Son & Father* to the Nat Brenner Scholarship Fund. Financial support for the benefit of students has also come from an ever-expanding list of charitable trusts, sometimes direct to individual applicants and, increasingly, through the School's management.

The School had a particularly difficult time in the early 1990s, when many talented people were deterred even from applying to theatre schools because of the exceptional problems they faced in finding the funds to pay the necessary fees (£6,600 a year at BOVTS in 1996) - and nearly as much again for living expenses, not to mention specialist requirements: 'On the first day of the first term, we were sent out to buy the equipment we would need for the course,' writes 1967-68 stage management student Jennifer Ellis. 'In my diary I record that I "didn't get all of it, but it cost £6.6s.1d." This may not seem much now (£6.30p) but it was more than two weeks' rent - a small fortune!'

For many students, financing their way through drama school in the 1990s has meant putting together a patchwork of money from savings, family, working part time during the course, scholarships, and an ingenious variety of sponsorship. But there was never a 'golden age' when the living and the grant-getting was easy for all. In 1946, it was just as problematic for some students to find fifteen guineas a term for a full time course, or even five guineas a term for evening classes. As incomes rose, so did costs: by 1957, these fees had doubled to thirty guineas, increasing tenfold in twenty years to £315 in 1977. Ten years later, they were over £1,000, and since 1994 have been over £2,000. Even when students were able to have their fees paid, they often had little help with living expenses. When Bob Harris came to BOVTS on its first ever Technical course in 1950, Newport in South Wales were willing to pay only the fees, so he had to continue living at home, which required a certain ingenuity as well as dedication: 'My parents paid for a rail season ticket, but the show often finished too late for me to get back to Newport, so I used to sleep in the Theatre Royal overnight, with the permission of Sid, the fire man. If there was a bed in the production - like in *Saint Joan,* the Dauphin's bed - I used to sleep on that. In *The Cocktail Party,* there was a psychiatrist's couch I used to bed down on. Sid would wake me up at about five o'clock and I'd catch a train at six, my mother would have my breakfast and sandwiches ready, and I'd catch a train to be back in the Theatre for rehearsals at ten o'clock and do it all again!'

Families are prepared to make great sacrifices to enable theatre students to train: some sold their 'luxuries' like cars and jewellery; others re-mortgaged or even sold their homes. Many students told extraordinary tales of how they raised the money to go to Theatre School: 'I wouldn't recommend having to dance with a python to earn your way through college,' laughs Pippa Haywood, who paid her rent for a year on the proceeds of a summer as a nightclub hostess in Corsica. Gabriel Prendergast heard that he'd been refused a New Zealand Drama Council bursary on the same day he received his letter of acceptance from BOVTS, but set off for England anyway. Arriving in Bristol six weeks before term started, he worked forty-one days out of forty-two hauling electric cable in a factory.

Although they were officially forbidden to take paid jobs during term time in the late 1950s and early 1960s, lots of BOVTS students worked at the Ashton Court Country Club (now Redwood Lodge): Edward Evanko sang there, under an assumed name; and some later top BBC producers were among its hostess/cigarette girls. Jenny Broughton was a waitress: 'We had a uniform with no pockets,' she recalls, 'so you had to keep the tips in your shoes. When my parents visited - satisfying themselves it wasn't a seedy nightclub - they said it must make walking awkward, but the more uncomfortable it was the better the waitresses liked it, because it meant we were better off!'

Countless BOVTS students have served customers in Bristol eateries - several of them as singing waiters. In the 1990s, Victoria Smurfit and Guy Lankester danced on tables as part of their job at an American 1950s-style restaurant. In the 1980s, Samantha Bond, Lisa Bowerman, Julia Ford and Bryan Kennedy were among those employed at a hamburger bar on College Green, performing a self-penned satirical cabaret in between serving, and earning less than £1 an hour for a seven-hour shift: 'We did pick up tips,' says Samantha, 'and from that day to this I've never left a restaurant without leaving a tip, however appalling the service was.'

There were many harrowing tales of illness caused by student poverty and youthful ignorance. People worked hard and ate badly: one girl lived on Shredded Wheat and baked beans until she was taken to hospital with suspected appendicitis that turned out to be constipation; young men survived on a diet of pasta and chips. Often they could not afford to heat their rented rooms. 'For the first two years I was working after School in bars and restaurants,' says Mark Negus-Bullock. 'It was all right most of the time, but at Christmas, when it got very busy, I was doing the *Nativity* tour, starting at quarter to seven and finishing at three, then I had a cleaning job at the School for a couple of hours, then I'd have a shower and have to be at the restaurant for six o'clock and work through till half one or two o'clock, get home about three and be back at the School for quarter to seven. I carried on working until Easter, when I collapsed with exhaustion, and was ill all through the holidays and into the summer term. So I stopped after that - and got into debt instead.' More and more Theatre School students have had to spend several years after they leave paying off debts and loans.

Professionally experienced teachers, housing advisers, lawyers, HGV truck drivers, musicians and dancers have been able to use their earlier skills part time to subsidise their expenses at the School. Generations of Technical students have worked as casuals on fit-ups or crewing at the Theatre Royal or the Hippodrome. But for many the only options are tiring low-paid jobs as supermarket shelf-stackers, night porters, factory hands, dressmakers, bar staff or theatre ushers. And the hours they spend earning the necessary pittance inevitably detract from the value of their training: 'The last thing I wanted to do was give up evenings and weekends to doing a low paid casual job when I had the opportunity to be using the facilities of the School,' says director Jeremy Meadow. 'I learnt television techniques and single camera video production, and spent many long and happy hours in the editing suite, gone midnight. If I'd had to earn my rent during the course, I would definitely have got less out of it.'

The School tries to help by offering needy students such jobs as cleaning, painting, and gardening, with one lucky man appointed as caretaker: Mark Lambert, Victor McGuire and Adrian Scarborough are just three of those who were able to live rent-free in an attic room at Downside Road in return for taking this responsibility for the building. One student used his keyboard skills to do typesetting for programmes; others have taken three hour Sunday classes with the BOVTS Youth Theatre; one particularly talented student was taken on as a poster designer; and each year the Bursar employs a student with computer experience.

In the early 1990s, as public funding became more and more difficult to obtain, Theatre School students became more enterprising. Among the most resourceful has been Martin Scott Gilmore who, having worked in the marketing department at Liverpool Playhouse, set about selling himself in the same professional way as he had been promoting shows. In a campaign spearheaded by a well-designed brochure, he invited people to 'Adopt An Actor' and become his patrons, receiving in exchange a regular newsletter updating them on his progress through a three year course. Damian Gaskin took the process a stage further, producing not only a regular newsletter for his sponsors but also T-shirts, mugs - and a booklet called *How To Raise £40,000 and Train At Theatre School,* which served the triple purpose of raising more funds, publicising the issue and helping future students.

'Friends at the Liverpool Playhouse advised me on how to market myself,' says Damian. 'I produced a leaflet with quotes from various directors I'd worked with and a few photographs. Then I mailed them to everybody I could think of:

family, friends, people I'd been at school or university with, all the Friends of the Liverpool Playhouse. It was a hard process, because it went along with what was really a glorified begging letter asking people to sponsor me for £20 a year. I know a lot of people didn't like it, but about a hundred and forty did, and were very generous, many of them giving much more.'

The financial difficulties students face at the Theatre School could at best be viewed as a realistic part of their preparation for a job which, for most, is insecure and low-paid. Eighty per cent of the members of the actors' trade union, Equity, are unemployed at any one time, and even those that do get work often have to wait weeks or months between jobs. Yet with the extraordinary determination and resilience that is characteristic of actors, they tend to look on the bright side, thinking of themselves as 'available for work' rather than 'resting' or 'unemployed', and taking up second-string careers like photography and writing, which can be fitted in between acting jobs.

Alan Collins left cost accountancy over thirty years ago to train as an actor, appeared in several BOV Company productions and on TV while still a student and was taken straight into the Company as an ASM: 'I may not have any money,' he says, 'but I have a treasure-chest of great memories.'

16. Nat Brenner, Principal of the Bristol Old Vic Theatre School 1963-1980.

Bristol Old Vic Theatre School 1946-1996

17. BOVTS in *The Voysey Inheritance* by Harley Granville Barker (University Drama Studio, spring 1965).

18. BOVTS in *All The World's A Stage* by Isaac Jackman (Little Theatre, May 1966).

19. Nat Brenner.

20. BOVTS in *The Winter's Tale* (University Drama Studio and Athenaeum Theatre, Plymouth, spring/summer 1967).

21. BOVTS in *Love's Sacrifice* by John Ford (Vandyck Theatre, November 1969).

22. BOVTS in *Make Me An Offer* by Wolf Mankowitz (Vandyck Theatre and Little Theatre, 1971).

23. BOVTS in *Make Me An Offer* by Wolf Mankowitz (Vandyck Theatre and Little Theatre, 1971).

24. BOVTS in *Elizabeth I* by Paul Foster (New Vic, December 1974).

25. Rudi Shelly.

12. Rudi Shelly: What is acting?

'Acting,' says Rudi Shelly, 'is the art of re-acting. It is playing. It is living. We are all acting all the time - the question is, do we want to do it in front of other people?' For Rudi, after fifty years' experience as tutor and mentor to performers in training, 'acting means trying, on ground of detailed text study, to teach people what to think with the mind of the character they are portraying. In other words, for me "acting" is another expression for "living". I call myself a movement instructor, but the question is, what do you mean by movement? We have a moving mind and imagination, a moving voice (and that means voice *and* speech) *and* we have a moving body. So it's the whole personality.'

'When I first came to the Theatre School,' says Danny Dryer, 'I fell into the trap of thinking I was going to learn to act. We were learning to dance and to speak properly and things like that, and I was waiting for the magic lesson to appear. It never did. It's nothing specific, it's a sort of process of osmosis - you absorb it as you go along.'

'A lot of the things you learn, it's hard to say exactly where they came from,' affirms Stephen Dillane. 'Acting is a process of self-discovery. All the Theatre School can do is prod people in the right direction. And it's not about the sum of the technical accomplishments, it's about finding your way to open yourself up in order to achieve a state in which those technical accomplishments will be of use to you.'

Says Ben Oldfield, 'The Bristol Old Vic School gives you all the skills and techniques you need as an actor, without impressing on you any specific methodology of "how to act". You're given lots of stimuli and ways to approach things but no specific route. You have to find out yourself, by trial and error, and by being intelligent and inquisitive. If you follow the teaching you're given, you should have all the faculties of good clear speech, voice projection, good posture, physical awareness - everything you need to be a good actor. It's like being a musician and learning scales. You have to do them - and keep on doing them - because without the basic means of expression you can't play a sonata or whatever, no matter how expressive and passionate you are.'

In Rudi Shelly, the Bristol Old Vic Theatre School has for half a century enjoyed an inspiring example of the passion, the discipline and the imagination that is fundamental to the actor - and to every other theatre worker. He has long described himself as 'a specialist in non-specialisation' and offered his pearls of wisdom (complete with the little grains of sand that make them stick) to anyone and everyone who came looking - and, even more important, listening - for them.

Regarded by generations of students as a sort of guru, commanding a mixture of respect and affectionate teasing, Rudi has shared his vast knowledge and consummate skill with all kinds of people, all over the world. Around Bristol, his restless energy and enthusiasm (not to mention the low pay) led him to engage in a wide range of out-of-School activities: teaching backward children and further-education adults; working with professional opera singers, amateur drama groups and patients at the Burden Neurological Institute; lecturing in prison and in university drama; talking to Army corps in barracks and to Townswomen's Guilds in church halls. Further afield, he has represented the BOV Theatre School at European conferences, and taken workshops and summer schools in Britain and abroad, from the Mozarteum in Salzburg to the Eugene O'Neill Centre in Connecticut, USA.

'At our first class he gave us a huge booklist, not necessarily about acting. From his wide travels and even wider reading he has built up an immense store of cultural knowledge, and seems to know everything about the theatre, art, architecture, customs and literature of every country in the world. And in such precise detail - he could tell you exactly when fashions changed, how people wore their hats, what sort of clothes they wore, or how they bowed in 1672 as opposed to 1673!'

Rudi is one of life's great communicators, very perceptive in his observations and incisive in his expression, 'but he always said himself that half of what he had to say was crap and half gold, and we had to suffer it all and find out which was which ourselves.' Emlyn Harris recalls a lesson when the entire group was suffering from boredom: 'We started to play killer - the game where one person attempts to murder everyone else in the room by winking at them - and, being actors, one by one the whole class died in spectacularly noisy and showy fashion. Rudi completely ignored the fact that his class was slumping to the floor around him and carried on regardless. But the next lesson, as our 'deaths' had been so terrible, he went into the finer details of dying on stage and, once the entire class was inert on the floor, left us where we were and went for a leisurely cup of tea.'

Rudi's training methods were evolved from reading the works of the great child psychologists, and his inspirational teaching has liberated the imaginations of generations of actors through a mixture of bullying and good humour: 'He has a ruthless and unsentimental approach to people, combined with an enormous insight,' says one student. 'He'll look at you, and see you for what you are without being swayed by any kindness. So he'll be completely blunt. And whether you like it or not he'll be right. Whether or not you can accept it at that point doesn't matter, because it stays in your head.'

Years after leaving the School, actors remember being told by Rudi that they had 'a quality of radiant amateurism', walked 'like a camel', stuck their chest out 'like a pregnant nightingale', or looked 'like an indecent proposal'. Sometimes his use of English as a foreign language would coin strange but remarkably accurate expressions: Valerie Wood has never forgotten Rudi's picturesque command to a rather fey chap in her class - 'Do not stand so private in your knees!'

Every actor who has passed through Bristol Old Vic Theatre School has several stories to tell about Rudi, and few can resist the temptation to echo his mid-European accent and recite some of his familiar catch-phrases. Rudi never discouraged students from imitating him, possibly because it meant those pearls of wisdom were repeated over and over even outside the classroom.

Some students despaired of the constant repetition that was always a feature of Rudi's teaching, but others came to believe it was a deliberate ploy to ensure that they could recall what he had said when they needed it later. Rudi himself would tell the students, 'You won't understand really anything I'm telling you here, but after seven years of working you will begin to understand'. Often it is long after leaving BOVTS that performers realise the enormous amount and usefulness of his advice: how to prepare thoroughly, how to get the most out of a script, how to make sense of classical texts, how to think laterally. Very many ex-students say that when they're waiting in the wings to go on stage they hear Rudi like a wise, cross-legged parrot on their shoulder, reminding them to stand up straight and to walk properly in such time-honoured phrases as 'Keep your pelvis quiet', 'Pull down your bolero ', and the most unforgettable of all - 'Squeeze your lemon'.

'What stays in my memory the most from this legendary movement teacher,' says Brian Blessed, 'is placing an imaginary lemon between the cheeks of my buttocks - the gluteus maximus, the muscle that holds up the anus - so that I would have correct deportment.'

'The genius of Rudi's teaching is that he encapsulates very important things with a memorable image - the idea of squeezing your lemon is so ludicrous that you will never forget it,' says Greg Doran. 'All the time I was directing *Titus Andronicus* (with Antony Sher in 1995) Rudi-isms kept coming to my mouth - phrases like "Don't play your red nose". He had this wonderful class where everyone would put on a red nose, and all the actors would lark about, playing up to it. Then Rudi would put one on what was already a rather large nose, and he would just carry on speaking in his normal voice, without playing the nose at all. And it was the funniest thing - this ludicrous business of having this red nose on his face while he was just talking about the weather or whatever. I didn't quite understand the relevance of it until much later in my career: there are scenes in *Titus,* for example, where there are quite ludicrous things happening, and rather than play up to that and tell the audience how funny you think those things are, you play absolutely dead serious against it, and then it is much, much funnier.'

Rudi's talent for fixing a useful hint forever in the back of the mind was illustrated time and again by students gleefully recounting the phrases he had indelibly stamped on their memory. For example, to cure the bad habit of looking downwards while on stage - without a purpose for so doing, Rudi planted the idea that the words **'DON'T LOOK HERE'** were painted in large red capitals on the floor. He suggested that students should always 'remember three very special members of the audience - one is blind, one is deaf, and the third can see and hear but cannot understand one word of your language, and you must make them all understand you'. And to protect them from the psychological dangers of really *feeling* the emotions of the character they played, he told them that no matter what they are doing on the outside, inside themselves actors 'must remain as cold as a polar bear's arse'.

Marc Sinden still goes to see Rudi if he has a problem theatrically that he can't work out, 'and he's infuriating because he comes up with the answer straight away! I was doing *Ross* at the Old Vic, we were rehearsing a long scene - about fifteen minutes - with Ross squatting and me standing over him, and I didn't know what to do with my hands. So I came down to Bristol and asked Rudi, and he said "Count eyelashes. Then you'll be concentrating on something else and your hands will hang naturally. Now do you want a cup of tea?"'

'What Rudi teaches you is common sense, but in a very entertaining way,' adds John Telfer. 'In *Hard Times,* I was playing a creepy Victorian character in a plotting scene, I had a big top hat, and we were sat round a table. During the technical rehearsal, I put the top hat on the table and started talking, when suddenly Rudi's voice rang into my mind from years before, saying "Don't ever put a top hat on a table between you. It's more beautiful than you are, and people will look at the top hat and not listen to what you're saying." So I put it on my knee out of the way.'

Rudi Shelly's wit and wisdom has been gathered into a book, edited by BOVTS graduate Simon Beresford with contributions from many ex-students: *Acting: The Gentle Art of Living Together.*

13. Actors in training

The original Bristol Old Vic Theatre School Acting courses advertised in 1946 were only three terms for full time students, though quite a few stayed on for a second year, which soon became the norm. A 1947 article in *Theatre World* outlined what the students learned: 'Subjects covered include voice production, breathing and relaxation, dialects, the method of learning a part, mime, the development of critical faculty and imaginative power. In addition there are special student productions, lessons in stage management, lectures from eminent theatrical personalities, and scenic design.' Each teacher had individual skills and strengths, but everybody taught everything, with the common aim of developing initiative, imagination and self-reliance in the students.

Until 1950, when the School accepted its first one-year stage management trainees, no distinction was made between student actors and student technicians. Even as late as the 1970s, most actors expected to begin their careers as ASMs in one of the regional theatres, and Bristol students in the 1940s learned what they needed to know by helping behind the scenes at the Theatre Royal, with some theory lessons from the Stage Director. After serving their time as extra hands backstage, actors would hope to be offered non-speaking 'walk-ons', then gradually work their way, if they were lucky and able, from small roles with only a few lines up to character roles, via the 'juve leads' (short for 'juvenile'), which were substantial parts for young people.

Several students from Edward Stanley's years tell of 'tears time' in the summer, when at least a third (sometimes nearly half) of them would be told they were unsuitable for the profession and could not come back for the second year, leaving perhaps twelve from a class of twenty. This policy of severely pruning the numbers continued under Duncan Ross: 'The end of the first year was a particular watershed. Looking back, and realising how finances worked, I think they took on far too many students in the first year knowing full well that they couldn't cope with that number in the second year. It was probably the only way of financing the School, but it was quite brutal.'

Since 1971, very few students have been asked to leave BOVTS before finishing their course: Nat Brenner used to say 'I take in that number of students who I believe can go into the profession, and some people who I think I can help'; and Chris Denys believes that 'to take someone off the street and say to them "I will train you as an actor" is saying to them "I think you *are* an actor, you could be a *good* actor, and I believe you could have an enjoyable and prosperous life *as* an actor". And that's a terrible thing to do to somebody unless you really believe it to be the case.'

One factor common to the training of actors throughout the fifty years at Bristol Old Vic Theatre School has been the process of ridding them of bad physical habits, idiosyncratic mannerisms and misleading attitudes, then rebuilding their confidence and competence through self-awareness and practical technique.

'When they arrive, full of intensity, humour and raw energy, they are suddenly asked to reconsider everything they've ever done in life,' explains Chris Denys. 'They have to think - "how do I walk? how do I talk? and how do I sit in a chair and get up again?" We're bringing those things into focus, because everything you do on stage has to have a reason. If you stand still and then make a gesture, the gesture means something. But if you're moving your arms about all the time, no gesture can mean anything. All those affectations and haphazard qualities have to be stripped away from them, so that they go through the embarrassment barrier and develop an extraordinary and often punishing level of awareness, both physical and emotional, of themselves and of other people.

'They can get very despondent and depressed round about February, but by March they start coming out of it, and by the end of the spring term they should be beginning to see a ray of light. Then as they go into the summer term they begin to enjoy it again, but by then they're aware of what they've got to do. At that stage it'll still be quite cerebral and there won't be a lot of passion in it because they're thinking about getting it right, but at least it'll begin to be entertaining. Gradually the technique becomes absorbed and invisible and they finish up being better structured performers - but the same personalities that we thought it worthwhile to take on in the first place.'

'You were made aware of every single idiosyncrasy you had - which was painful but necessary,' says one student. 'It's like if you have an abscess, you've got to get rid of the tooth and the pus or else it'll never heal - we had to do the same thing to our entire physical mechanism (the way we moved) and to our brains (the way we thought and expressed ourselves) so that we could be totally objective about the way we did things and how our system worked.'

'You felt a lot of the time that you were constantly being criticised, all the worst things about you were being laid bare in front of you,' says another. 'You had to remind yourself that you were there in the first place because they believed you could be a good actor. After all, they had chosen you from hundreds of applicants.'

'The first year was an immense shock, because I realised how little I did know about me, and the way I moved, and my bad habits, and my voice,' admits a third. 'There's so much involved that you begin to wonder if three years will be enough! We listened in June to a recording of how our voices had been when we arrived the previous September, and there was an amazing difference: I used to talk incredibly quickly but they really slowed me down and made me appreciate how you have to take your time with language to get the imagery; and my voice is far more rooted, it flows more and has a better tone.'

Throughout the first year, Acting students are constantly presented with new challenges alongside an exhausting and repetitive regime of daily movement and voice exercises. The intense concentration on themselves is balanced by encouraging them to make a careful study of others. Duncan Ross's students had a regular class called 'obs-ex' - short for 'observation exercises' - for which they watched not just people, but animals too. Generations of students have taken the short trip along the Downs from the Theatre School to Bristol's Zoo, returning to use the experience in animal improvisations, one of many ways used to develop imagination and a capacity for quick-thinking. Students also remember being asked to present themselves as 'a policeman's whistle being blown', 'an old boot flapping', or 'a tube of toothpaste'. They were hairbrushes for Duncan Ross, leaves in a fog for Rudi, and sea anemones for John Hartoch. Douglas Dempster took the Improvisation classes in the 1960s and early 1970s: 'It did result in some very courageous jumps into the unknown, because improvisation cultivates a willingness to make a fool of yourself, what Nat used to call the "performing seal" aspect of the actor - you have to learn to disregard what others say about you in the process of learning to act.'

You also have to learn what's involved in different styles and periods of theatre, usually through 'acting exercises', often with guest directors, working on selected scenes (or condensed versions of whole plays) that cover the range of the classic repertoire, from medieval to 20th century: *Everyman,* Shakespeare, Restoration, 18th century (*She Stoops to Conquer* and *The Rivals*); Shaw, Ibsen, Chekhov, Wilde; Peter Barnes, Tom Stoppard, David Hare, C P Taylor, Alan Ayckbourn and Alan Bennett - as well as new scripts written specially for the students. John Hartoch has adapted classics such as *The Jungle Book* and *The Three Musketeers,* and was commissioned in 1994 to create a play about the dangers of drugs: *Wheel of Fortune* was originally performed in schools by a student cast and later became a professional project involving BOVTS graduates in both live touring and a schools' video.

Textwork for actors is not an academic study: you don't get it right or wrong, you just have to think about it: 'One year we did two versions of a shortened *Twelfth Night,* one as a romance and the other as a cynical black comedy,' says Douglas Dempster. 'This fed both groups, because by watching each other work, they came to understand how the same text could yield two completely divergent results.'

Dozens of ex-students could go on for hours about Rudi's classes on the opening of Chekhov's *The Seagull:* 'Before Medvedenko could say, "Why do you always wear black?" Rudi would have investigated the whole scene - how you come on to the stage, what it's all about, what the characters are doing, what they're coming on with - before that first line of the play would be able to be said,' says one; 'And Masha would reply "I am in mourning for my life" - that is, I'm unhappy,' adds another. 'We'd do that scene and spend an hour on six lines. The next class we wouldn't get any further, because Rudi had so much to say about it - the interplay and the subtext and all that.'

'Rudi's famous expression is "It's all in the text - ducky"!' says Sara Markland. 'An actor studying text is like a detective, rooting through the script, finding clues all the time.' Nevertheless, as Jenny Seagrove has found, 'It's all very well to say "It's all in the text" when you're dealing with Chekhov and Shakespeare, but it's not always useful to go back to the text and break it down, because sometimes you don't get very good texts, so you have to fill them out. When you get a real piece of rubbish - which I've done plenty of - you really have to be inventive. You have to imagine whole worlds for these characters and imbue them with something else, and that's where it really tests you.'

Eventually, the day comes when student actors have the chance they've been waiting and working for: to get out there in front of an audience and do it! The choice of plays for full-scale production is limited by the need to have large casts and lots of parts that are substantial enough to allow each actor to be challenged. Sometimes directors devise a theatrical collage so that as many as seventeen actors all have something worthwhile to do. Elwyn Johnson and Neil Rhoden did this in 1983 with a memorable musical of the 1920s and 1930s called *Blowin' The Blues Away.*

There have always been showcase performances in the Theatre Royal for the summer leavers, with agents and potential employers invited from London. Edward Stanley's students did only one public production, at the end of their two year course, though most students then had experience in BOV Company shows. In 1951, the graduates showed off their talents with just two weekday matinées of three short pieces, each directed by a different member of the staff: Lady Gregory's *The Dragon* by Edith Manvell; Scenes from *Hamlet* by Anthony Holland; and Saroyan's *Subway Circus* by Stanley himself.

Duncan Ross courageously challenged students with several plays which were performed only by the most avant-garde companies in the 1950s, including Ionesco's *Jacques* and *The Star* by Yvonne Mitchell. And Nat Brenner presented his graduates in a repertoire of shows, sometimes as many as four productions in one week. Whereas Michel Saint-Denis, who had fewer students, used to present the same cast in two different plays - to give them as wide a variety of styles as possible - Nat Brenner used to do the same play with two different casts, to spread the good parts and give more students a chance to show off their talents. There were two productions a term, and only one group of students in each, with the actors alternating between major and minor roles. Under this system Jenny Seagrove shared the part of Desdemona in *Othello* with Miranda Richardson; Jack Klaff and John Telfer doubled as King Arthur in *The Quest;* and in *The Italian Straw Hat,* three actors shared the lead: Richard Howard, Richard Frost and Jeremy Child.

Parts in the public shows are considered an integral part of the training: 'They stretch you,' says Tony Howes. 'I'm a working class lad, so I could easily do Billy in *Billy Liar,* so they'd give me Algernon in *The Importance of Being Earnest* instead and I'd have to find a way that I could do that. It's not good casting, but it stretches you as an actor'; 'We had to do the *Meg and Mog Show* and I was given Meg, but I didn't want to do it,' says Dariel Pertwee. 'I had to sing, dance and act all at the same time, which to me at the time was an absolute nightmare. But it was invaluable, because it really taught me that having done that, I could do anything.' Three years after leaving BOVTS, Dariel was on the Theatre Royal stage singing and dancing with the best of them in the Bristol Old Vic pantomime.

'The shows we put on in King Street in June are intended to make everyone look enormously talented and eminently employable,' says Chris Denys. '*Mansfield Park* was an obvious choice for the Theatre Royal in 1995 because of the revival of interest in adaptations of Jane Austen for mini-series on television, and the massive market for costume melodrama, which is increasing because it makes money and raises American capital. *Red Noses,* which we did in the New Vic, is ideal for a presentation because it's brilliantly written, a wonderful script, so on the one hand it's demonstrating their ability to cope with very literate, complicated and funny English text - which shows they can play Shakespeare or Shaw or John Osborne or Berkoff - and on the other hand it makes use of their tumbling, juggling, mime and clowning skills, which demonstrates their sense of comic timing and their ability to play an audience.'

Some students were lucky enough to have professional experience of acting even before they finished their course. When Anthony Holland did a summer season at Cromer in 1951, BOVTS students Norman Rossington, Susan Dowdall, Kenneth Cope and Phyllida Law joined him for an eye-opening experience of weekly rep. Kenneth Cope remembers 'we had these "cue scripts", which were dreadful - you'd just get the last word from the previous person's speech and you didn't know how long or short the speech was!' And, Norman Rossington recalls, 'We did a play called *Love's A Luxury,* in which Ken played my son, and we used to go on not knowing the second act - we used to just make it up. That was wonderful training!'

If feature films were being made locally, the Theatre School would often provide actors - or crowds: Pat Armstrong was Hayley Mills' stand-in on *Tiger Bay* (1959); as first years, the class of '74 were in *The Wicker Man,* impersonating what was supposed to look like 'a Buddhist ritual' in Somerset's Wookey Hole, and creating an amusing (and inaccurate!) 'solicitor in nude film shock' story for a front page news item about Leslie Perrin many years later. Students at the School in March 1965 were used as extras in the pop film *Catch Us If You Can:* 'Nat Brenner made Norman Eshley and me appear in drag as "Jean Harlow" figures,' recalls Brian Austin. 'Wandering around Bath in drag with the local Rugby Club around was interesting, and the Dave Clark Five's agent had a fit when he found his lads talking to two transvestites!'

When Daniel Hill was only in his second term, the BBC rang the School and asked if there was anyone there who came from Bristol and had an Equity card. They needed a boy to act with Albert Finney in a play called *Forget-Me-Not-Lane* by Peter Nichols, who had himself trained as an actor at BOVTS in the 1940s: 'Nat let me go up for it, but when I was offered the job, he said if I took it, I'd have to leave the School. When I said I'd rather turn it down and carry on with my training, he said I could do both - but told me if I'd said anything different, he'd have chucked me out!' Years later, Victoria Smurfit also worked with Albert Finney while still a student at BOVTS, on the 1994 feature film *The Run of the Country,* also written by a former Bristol student, Shane Connaughton.

What is clear from the experience of most ex-students is that the two or three years spent at the Theatre School were only the first part of an actor's training, during which 'You're like a huge sponge, soaking up lessons that you only learn to apply later'.

14. Move that body: let's get physical

The actor's body is the main tool of the trade and needs to be both well-maintained and well-trained. Getting fit is only the start of it. Even such simple actions as standing up and sitting down have to be re-learned as consciously controlled actions because 'your body language tells us what you're driven by and says as much as the words that you're speaking'. All of the main Movement teachers at Bristol Old Vic Theatre School - Rudi Shelly since 1946, Lynn Britt from 1965 to 1980, Aubrey Budd since 1981, and Gail Gordon since 1984 - have trained and worked as dancers. Gail Gordon also worked as a contortionist!

'We obviously can't turn everyone into dancers - though we don't do badly. Three of our graduates were in *A Little Night Music* at the National Theatre: Brendan O'Hea, Paul Kynman and Joanna Riding - who also starred in *Carousel* and *Me and My Girl*. Pinky Amador went straight from the School into *Miss Saigon*,' says Gail, who choreographs all of the School shows and some for the BOV Company, for which she also provides young dancers for the annual pantomime from her own local school. 'Most students come here with no idea at all of how the body functions, and what we aim to do is create a bodily awareness which is going to help the acting: making them feel comfortable in their bodies, and aware of what they're doing, so they don't have any little twitches and funny things that distract.'

'Some students arrive at the School having never even done a forward roll in their life,' adds stage combat teacher Jonathan Howell. 'I try to teach them basic acrobatic/gymnastic movements, Geoffrey Buckley shows them basic mime, and Gail has to train them in basic dance movements. We're all coming from different sides, but we're all aiming at the same thing, which is movement that they can use on the stage - eventually. They may not see it like that while they're here, because it doesn't appear to be directly useful. Unless, of course, they end up doing *Salad Days*. Then they have to do time-steps and step-ball changes - and even forward rolls!'

Many of Robin Herford's classmates were quite athletic and sporty, 'but it was quite strange how one form of physical co-ordination and grace didn't always convert into another. People who could star on the football field could look very silly in a pair of tights!'

Theatre School mornings begin for actors with 'limbers' - a twenty-minute physical and vocal warm-up. Strenuous exercise for an hour or two every day can come as a shock to the system when they start their training. Some smiled and others winced to remember their first week of Movement classes, when it was quite common to see students making their way upstairs from the basement studio on their bums because their legs ached so much: 'You discover bits of body you didn't know you had until they began to throb!'

'The first two terms were really hard. There was a lot of muscle-twitching sort of dance, jumping up and down for hours on end. A lot of people who had never danced before found it extraordinarily difficult being put into all sorts of positions they'd never imagined their bodies would go in.' But the motto has always been 'Don't say "Can't do it", say "Can't do it - YET",' and after a few weeks, the effort begins to pay off: 'I'd been rather fat and plump for years, done no exercise and certainly wasn't a dancer,' admits Nicholas Blane, who later played a leading role in *42nd Street* at Drury Lane. 'But towards the end of the first term, I was walking down the street one day, when I suddenly felt as if all my limbs and muscles were free, in a way that I hadn't felt since I was a child. I felt very loose and free - thanks to the Movement classes.'

Rudi always stresses how well children use their bodies, before social pressures overcome natural instincts. He encourages the students to reflect on how their grown-up bodies have changed, by observing the healthy movements babies make without thinking - before self-consciousness sets in and people start to mumble and slouch rather than stand up straight and yell.

For Rudi, 'movement', like 'acting', is another expression for 'living'. Good posture is a fundamental starting point: 'When you come here you've got terrible posture -

everybody has,' says one recent graduate. 'But Rudi makes you stand how you should stand, which at first is very uncomfortable because you're not used to it, you're used to slouching around. He makes you stand like that for an hour, and breathe properly, doing some very basic movements, and it's surprisingly tiring.'

Rudi always had a host of typically memorable expressions to nudge people into proper posture: 'If you tell someone to stand up straight, they usually just stick their shoulders out. You're much more likely to do it right if you think of "squeezing your lemon", or imagine yourself as a roller towel - if you pull down at the back, you'll go up at the front!' smiles David Straun who, like many actors-turned-teachers, finds himself using what he learned from Rudi with his own students.

From the late 1940s to the early 1960s, first year Acting students started every day with an unforgettable limbering-up class with Rudi which began with 'extremely rigorous' PT-style exercises to the sound of Waldteufel's *Skater's Waltz,* often outdoors in the Saint Nicholas School courtyard. Sometimes the students were asked to make up their own words to the famous tune - one way of training them to speak clearly while moving around the stage. Sometimes the lyrics were extremely rude! One year they were delightfully simple: 'Here is a tale, sad to relate. There once was a whale who just longed to skate'. Another they were witty and inventive, full of references to the teachers and the course, with the odd sideways swipe at Rudi's characteristic comments, italicised in this little extract:
'Here at the School, we love each rule
We dig our movement, it's real cool (*keep your pelvis quiet*)
Can't do it - yet, but we'll not fret
Keep smiling, darlings, you're not dead yet .....
We're not competing with Sadler's Wells feeting
But he keeps repeating *"Your heels should be meeting"*
We would if we could - but we're no bloody good.'

Student actors were asked to do so many inexplicable things that they learned to accept instruction without question, and later discovered surprising practical purposes to the most obscure exercises: 'You would spend ages with a bamboo stick, moving it in certain ways around your head and back, and Rudi would never tell us what the hell we were doing. Until one day weeks later, he told us to bring our rehearsal capes in - and we had to do the same movements as we had with the bamboo cane. And what he had taught us was how to put on a cloak without taking off the wig of the person standing next to you on stage.'

'Rudi does a very funny lesson on fans. He closes the fan - because, he says, you never open your fan unless you wish to upstage your leading lady - and says "You do to the fan whatever you'd like to do to the person you're talking to". Which can either be very sexy or very violent, but always makes it much more interesting to watch.'

Rudi taught not only *how* to move in a certain way, but also *why:* if, for example, you live in a large castle, you have to speak up and make grand gestures or no-one will take any notice of you; similarly, people stand apart with their arms outstretched in Restoration comedy, waving fans and handkerchiefs about, 'Because they stink, darling. They don't bath'!

Tim Pigott-Smith remembers 'Rudi told us "When you're doing Elizabethan or Jacobean drama, you have to lift your arms up from the shoulder, not from the elbow". And you'd think - what a stupid thing to say. But just imagine the person on stage playing a king who lifts his arms up from the elbow - what a prat he looks! When you lift them up from the shoulder, as Rudi used to say, you're addressing not just the Elizabethan world, but the universe - and eternity.'

Lynn Britt joined the Theatre School in 1965 to assist Rudi, and worked alongside him 'for fifteen glorious years shared with colleagues who inspired and had a unified concept of training'. At BOVTS, she explains, 'I developed a choreographic palette of "walking into dance styles" covering every area of dance specialisation, whereby the actors experienced tap to jazz to contemporary in relation to given plays and musicals. Through techniques involving relaxation, slow motion, stillness and the breath, they acquired a well-functioning, toned and flexible body with a "divine spine", and assimilated all the disciplines of body awareness and dance styles.'

'She was marvellous at making actors who had two left feet look as though they could move,' says Kim Hicks. 'She could design simple moves and teach people to do them with a bit of panache so that they could look for a moment as though they were Fred Astaire!'

'The physical training we got at the BOV School stays with you all your life,' adds Teresa Campbell. 'You're not likely ever to be complacent about how your body works, and you'll try to keep it in shape.'

When Chris Denys became Principal, the students had classes with various Movement teachers (among them Tutte Lemkow - who was the Fiddler in the original *Fiddler on the Roof*) until the autumn of 1981 when classically trained Sadler's Wells dancer Aubrey Budd joined the School, leaving three years later to join a London production of *42nd Street,* and later returning to teach part time alongside Gail Gordon: 'We do a little bit of everything,' says Aubrey. 'Basic ballet, historical dances like the gavotte and minuet, tap, history of dance, jazz, national dancing. Not everybody is cut out to be a dancer, it's more about co-ordination and a sense of well-being. People are surprisingly unco-ordinated: I say to them, you don't walk with the same arm as leg, and you don't dance with the same arm as leg. But as soon as they try to dance and put movement to music, they automatically do the same arm as leg! Very strange.'

'Most of the students haven't done anything like this before, so I have to start from scratch, teaching posture, dance, tap dance and presentation of songs,' adds Gail Gordon, who has introduced a scheme of dance projects which the first year students have to present within the School at the end of each term. It's not about showing off as dancers, more about demonstrating an ability to work as a team and, for some, a willingness to tackle an uncongenial task.

Many students testify that such willingness was often called on in the late 1950s after Duncan Ross replaced ballet classes at the School of Dancing with compulsory Saturday morning judo lessons. These were taught by brown belt George Brandt, a lecturer at Bristol University Drama Department, who became a regular visiting teacher at the Theatre School between 1955 and 1966: 'Bill Ross's idea was that judo was a good discipline in itself, in terms of balance, and reaction speeds. But also he wanted to have good stage fights, and I arranged one or two fights for him, and for the Bristol Old Vic. I remember one day Annette Crosbie and another student, Patricia Healy, decided to send me up and pretend, after a vigorous bout, to be seriously damaged. It was a marvellously acted little drama, designed to alarm me - but I don't think I was fooled for very long,' says George, whose most outstanding student was Brian Blessed, one of the few who kept it up after leaving the School. Quite a few students disliked doing judo, and didn't know why it was part of the course. One thought 'the idea was that we would all be toughened up' - but George Brandt explains that 'It was about learning to relax and respond. If you tense up, you lose your responses. The thing about judo is that the moment you are in trouble you have to relax your way out of it, which is a good parallel for acting'.

'It does help people to relax under stress, to retain good posture, to breathe in a more relaxed way, and generally to meet the stress of performance,' adds Jerry Hicks, who was area coach for the West of England and Chairman of the British Judo Association's national coaching committee, and took over as the School's judo teacher for two years before it was dropped from the timetable in 1968. 'The students would learn to fight in a way that looked convincing on the stage, and to perform pre-arranged moves with a partner, that look as real as possible. But there were much more fundamental reasons for teaching judo to actors. Certain mental-physical disciplines in judo are very much related to Zen Buddhist training, and could be just as helpful to an actor as to a fighter.'

'Judo classes were frightening,' recalls Edward Evanko. 'You had to let yourself free fall and you'd get headaches if you didn't do it correctly. And I didn't do it correctly many times! But thirty years later, when I did the Peter Brook *Carmen* at Lincoln Centre in New York, some little memory of these judo lessons came back because we had a lot of fighting to do, and one of the main things about fighting on stage is that you must be relaxed or else you hurt yourself or your partner.'

On fine days, passers-by often see students fighting in the Theatre School car park, or across the road on the grassy Downs - but it's not for real. Though the weapons look genuinely dangerous, no-one gets hurt because every move is aimed at the stage, and it's all carefully controlled. Fencing has always been part of the course, not only because it's needed for period roles from Shakespeare to swashbuckling, but because it helps to sharpen the reflexes, and develop concentration. In the 1940s and early 1950s, there were weekly fencing sessions with

Anthony Holland, who held competitions within the School and encouraged students to join the Proscenium fencing team and enter the West of England foil fencing championships. Some of the men had already learned fencing while in the army and were highly skilled; and most of the women thoroughly enjoyed it too. A succession of fencing teachers followed: a military man who also taught the boys at Clifton College in the later 1950s; former Olympic standard 'Professor' John Field until the late 1960s; then Douglas Dempster, who had himself been taught at Rose Bruford by an Olympic fencing coach. In the 1970s, there was one who irritated some of the students because he 'used to go on about stabbing the girls in their "Bristols",' and another with one arm, which was rather unnerving!

Jonathan Howell has been in charge of stage combat at BOVTS since the summer of 1988. He teaches several different historical styles of sword play - for example rapier and dagger from the Elizabethan period, and single sword for Restoration - as well as quarterstaff 'stick work' and a pot pourri of unarmed combat ranging from basic gymnastics and acrobatics up to punches, kicks, throws and miniature wrestling, with a bit of oriental martial-arts-style movement. Since the formation of the Society of British Fight Directors in 1969, all but a very few students at the end of their first year of training have taken the Performance Certificate in Stage Fighting, for which they have to learn a four-minute routine involving rapiers, daggers and hand-to-hand fighting within a piece of dialogue.

'Fighting is like a dialogue,' says Jonathan, who studied stage fighting while training as a dancer at Guildford, and worked professionally first as a dancer in ballet and opera companies in Britain and abroad, then as an actor, choreographer, director, fight arranger and teacher. 'You have moments when it's a slow conversation, others when it's fast-moving. Sometimes there's a statement and no answer, or a pause before you get the answer. And everything is applied to theatre, so you always have to remember to make sure you look good in the scene. The whole thing is an illusion: you have to convince the audience that something is happening when it really isn't. So you have to learn to fight with a cool interior even if you're emoting wildly on the outside!'

Years ago, emoting wildly was way out of fashion:

'Before the 1960s, English actors were always well known for acting from the neck upwards - beautiful speaking voices, but not much going on down below!' says regular guest teacher Geoffrey Buckley, a mime artist who hails from Lancashire and trained with Eduardo de Filippo in Italy and Jacques Lecoq in Paris. Ex-students gleefully imitate him explaining moves with French words but in a Northern accent: 'You don't do it like that, lad, do it like this - comme ça'!

'As playwrights like Pinter and Thornton Wilder emerged, writing plays that relied as much on movement as on words, we got more into physical shows,' explains Geoffrey. 'And since that theatrical revolution, it's become even more physical: lots of actors are working out in the community and in education with very low budgets, so they can't always afford lots of props and sets and have to make it work by the way they move; and there are more and more companies working in "physical theatre", so we're getting more and more adventurous in what we can do with our bodies.'

With Edith Manvell, Isabel Chisman and Edward Stanley in the 1940s, students practised 'occupational mime': pretending to plane a piece of wood, or sell tickets on a bus, or pass an imaginary unidentified object round the group. With Geoffrey Buckley in the 1990s, 'It's the dramatic side of movement we work for. Unlike dance, where the movement flows much more, we work in isolations and disassociations - finger, body, a bit at a time. When people pick their leg up, their arm very often automatically moves as well, but they learn to isolate certain parts of the body while they move others, and the disassociation part of it is breaking down the movements. Then we work on the mime techniques - opening a door, picking something up, or moving in a particular style, like a robot, or an animal.'

There are classes of two or three hours 'getting physical' - doing press ups, and somersaults and standing on your hands, working the body that's been loosened up by the basic dance and fitness routines. Then the classes move on to using masks and acting out basic Commedia scenarios, or selected scenes from plays: 'With masks,' explains Geoffrey Buckley, 'we start with a neutral one that makes you use your body to express emotions that you would have shown more on your face in everyday life.

Then we move on to an expressive mask - a half-mask, so the actor can speak as well, and has to find the right voice to suit the character of the mask. It can be quite dangerous if you don't know what you're doing, because it releases emotions in the body. There's never only one character in a mask - it depends on the person who's interpreting it. And one person can get as many as fifteen different interpretations from a single mask, either playing to the character, or against it - if it's a happy mask, behaving sadly, as an obvious example. And that's a way of feeling your way into what it's like to be somebody else, a completely different character.'

Versatility is still highly valued at BOVTS, because the more skills actors have the more employable they are. Over the years, students in the summer term have had a go at gymnastics, roller skating, trampolining, car driving and juggling, and a chance to try their hand at puppetry (ex-students have done well out of *Spitting Image* and the Muppets) and their 'seat' at horseriding.

One apparently unlikely subject on the regular timetable is yoga, first introduced in the 1960s by Lynn Britt and now taught by Lynette Erving, who trained as an actor and teacher at Rose Bruford (with her husband Francis Thomas) and joined the BOVTS staff in 1981: 'There's a very definite connection between the body, the breath and the mind,' says Lynette, who also teaches Voice classes. 'Yogic breathing and chanting can be very useful for voice, and I use bits of the yoga movement in my Voice classes. I don't go into the spiritual aspects, I'm concerned with focus, concentration, awareness - all of which are so important for the actor. And in showing them a movement and asking them to do it, I'm echoing what a director is doing all the time, though - unlike dance - it doesn't have the element of performance in it, only the movement discipline.'

15. Out of the mouths of actors: voice, speech, singing - and music

'Just in the way a dancer trains every muscle of the body, you can look at and train separately the various aspects of speaking,' explains Lynette Erving. 'Speech is movement, a highly complex series of movements - of the breathing, of the larynx, inside the larynx, all the shapings of the lips and the tongue. But we take it for granted because we learnt it as children. There is a time, which is in the training, for looking at it in a self-conscious way. And then there is a time for forgetting that, in performance, or in everyday communicating.'

Actors not only have to be heard at the back of a big theatre without shouting, but also have to ensure that they still *have* a voice after perhaps eight performances a week for weeks at a time: 'I've had a tired voice, but I've never lost it,' says Eamon Boland, even when 'we were doing two-and-a-half hour shows twice a day, and if you hadn't learnt the techniques of basic diaphragm breathing, then you *would* lose your voice.'

'Diaphragm' is not a word found very often in everyday life, and many students arrive at the Theatre School with no idea what it is, let alone where. Not for long. The English word comes from two Greek ones meaning 'across' and 'fence', which is quite a good description of the dome-shaped muscle underneath the lungs that is attached to the breastbone at the front and the lower spine at the back. When you breathe in, the diaphragm contracts, pulling air into the lungs. When you breathe out, the diaphragm relaxes, pushing up against the lungs and forcing air out.

Ken Woodward went to his first Voice Production class in the 1940s, expecting to learn how to speak: 'But we never said a word! We were taught how to breathe from the diaphragm rather than the upper chest. We took it in turns to lie on the floor, and the person you were working with would press on your diaphragm to make you breathe properly, with their other hand on your upper chest to make sure you weren't doing the wrong sort of breathing. And then you did that to your partner - who was usually a girl because there were only three men and nine women!'

The Voice teaching of Edward Stanley and Edith Manvell (occasionally joined, in the 1940s, by Dartington voice teacher Leonard Bennett) was based on 'the Behnke method', detailed in a book called *The Technique of Good Speech* by Kate Emil-Behnke, whose family had a long tradition of voice training. Now considered very old-fashioned, developing 'the Behnke diaphragm' did not suit everyone. Some felt they benefited from the emphasis on 'breathing as nature intended you to, as babies do when they're born'. Some found it gave them 'a bit of a paunch - a big muscle just below the rib cage'. Others were puzzled or amused: 'You were supposed to breathe in at the same time as speaking - I nearly asphyxiated!' says Gwenllian Davies; 'You couldn't do it properly unless you had your spine level with the floor, which seemed virtually impossible, and probably is,' adds Antony Tuckey, recalling that 'The Behnke method was full of unintentional humour: you had to lie on the floor, take a deep breath and then do your "let go"' - which Kenneth Cope laughingly describes as 'lessons in farting'.

Breathing properly was only one element in the 'speech gym' exercises introduced by Duncan Ross, which also encouraged students to concentrate equally on what they were saying and what they were doing: 'We learned bits of poetry or prose - things like "They went to sea in a sieve" - which we had to repeat as we went round a sort of obstacle course: walking along benches, climbing up frames, vaulting over hurdles.'

Daphne Heard also took classes in verse-speaking - without the obstacle course. In the late 1950s, when the Principal's family lived at the School, young Joanna Ross had a cat called Lavender, which was sometimes brought into the classroom: 'Young students had very little grasp of the slow and patient pursuit of a beloved in 17th century poetry, so Daphne would get them to hold Lavender and address their feelings to her,' says Maggie Collins, remembering that many years later Lavender would still respond knowingly to the rhythms of those verses.

Kathleen Stafford, who taught Voice and Speech at BOVTS from the late 1950s to the mid-1970s, lived with her sister in the nearby village of Backwell, where they founded the Playhouse Theatre, and used to put on productions with BOVTS students alongside local amateurs. In his first year at the School, Mark Buffery played Petruchio in Miss Stafford's *Taming of the Shrew:* 'She knew her Shakespeare inside out - and she cut out all the naughty bits!' says Mark. 'Because of Katy I've always played to the little old lady in the back row who's partially deaf: Katy's hearing wasn't terribly good and she used to take us to the Hippodrome and sit up in the gallery while we had to "whisper" speeches on the stage that she could hear.'

'It was perhaps no bad thing for a Voice teacher to be rather deaf,' adds Rob Edwards. 'At least you always had to speak up! Katy's lesson might involve repeating lists of words concentrating on certain lip or tip of tongue consonants - lip, pip, wit, nit, etc - and the game for the lads was to substitute rude homonyms which she didn't catch, of course, because of her deafness. Or did she? Such was the level of sophisticated wit.'

Allison Hancock remembers Jack Ritz bringing to Katy's lesson a poem with the F word in it, then losing his nerve and mumbling: 'What was that again, Jack?' said Katy, 'Fuck? did you say? Well for heaven's sake, let's hear it then. A nice open U, come on, now open that mouth! And a good sharp K, that's it, let it really EXPLODE off your tongue. Come on, all together, FUCK. And again. Excellent!'

Many students affectionately referred to Miss Stafford as 'dear Katy', describing her variously as 'an elegant actress dowager-lady of the old school', 'a genteel Edith Evans' and 'the Cicely Berry of Bristol'. Her manner and methods were mostly remembered as very traditional: 'she used to try to get everybody to speak like John Gielgud, because she thought that was the way actors should speak', but also 'very friendly, as if one were having lessons in her private drawing room with tea and cucumber sandwiches'.

When illness forced Katy Stafford to retire, several ex-students (among them David Calder, Stephanie Cole and Marion Reed) taught Voice at the Theatre School until Maggie Ross, described as 'a young Scottish socialist with incredible vitality' joined the staff in 1976. Two years later, Francis Thomas arrived. Hailed by dozens of ex-students as a genius, with a 'delightfully dry' sense of humour and a voice 'like melted pure chocolate', he had been a young actor at Liverpool Rep and later a mature student at Rose Bruford, where he trained as both a teacher and an actor, combining both jobs before eventually focusing on the teaching. Though he originally concentrated on Voice and Speech at BOVTS, he also supervises the Theatre-In-Education work, drawing on his experience as leader of a T-I-E team in London.

Gone are the days of the elocution lessons that made everybody sound like an old-fashioned BBC broadcaster. As Voice teachers, Francis Thomas and Lynette Erving share an eclectic approach to the subject. What's most important is speaking clearly, for which students need to understand and practise the very precise movements of the mouth that make each particular sound.

'We do muscle exercises,' says Francis, 'pulling funny faces and tight smiles, limbering up the muscles of the lips and tongue. Then we do sound drills - things like "dubba-dubba-dubba" - that lead up to connected speech in tongue-twisters.' Prompted to recall these drills, students would go into well-practised recitals of such surprisingly useful gobbledegook as 'Babbety, bebbety, bibbety, bobbety, bubbety. Kakkety, kekkety, kikkety, kokkety, kukkety. Gaggety, Geggety, Giggety, Goggety, Guggety' or tongue-twisters like 'Give me the gift of a grip-top sock, A dip-drape, ship-shape, tip-top sock, Not your spiv-slick, slap-stick, slip-slop sock, But a plastic elastic grip-top sock' and 'What a to-do to die today At a minute or two to two, A thing distinctly hard to say But a harder thing to do. For they'll beat a tattoo at two today, A rat-tat-tat too, at two, And the dragon will come When he hears the drum, At a minute or two to two today, At a minute or two to two'.

Francis has endeared himself to students by making the repetitive processes fun: 'Every class, you knew you were going to go through a whole series of vocal exercises that were - as with any art you're practising - fundamentally a bore,' says one, 'but he would be very meticulous, and at the same time he had such an impish manner that you would enjoy these tedious routines'; 'He'd have fifteen different possibilities for every part of the lung you were going to expand to fill it with air! So each class was different and new,' says another.

It's all aimed at what Voice teacher Dennis Blakelock called 'careful carelessness' - making clear speech sound right without looking forced: 'It should look care-less, but it needs to be care-full,' says Francis. 'Like a wonderfully accurately executed tap dance, where everything is tapping at the right time, with the right pressure, at the right beat of music for the right length of time. And it looks so effortless - not so deliberate that you can see the poor soul going through all the torments of hell to get their feet in the right place.'

Neville Watchurst recalls a class outdoors on the Downs, when Francis 'described, in his beautifully measured, gentle voice, how he wanted us to run up and release a "bowling ball of sound". He then demonstrated the technique - stunning several passing pigeons and knocking two old ladies off a bench a hundred yards away!'

Francis and Lynette provide a very firm basis of 'received pronunciation' ('R P' for short - what people sometimes call 'proper' English), but work towards enhancing the actors' potential range rather than eliminating their natural accents. Being able to speak in several regional accents was an important skill for rep actors who expected to play a wide range of characters. Performers are now more likely to be cast in parts using their natural accent, but students still learn the basics they need to be aware of when working in a different one - like how useful it is to look as well as listen to the way people speak: 'The best way to learn an accent,' says Francis Thomas, 'is to go to the area where it's used. Sometimes an accent might sound rather flat, but when you see it, there's a lot of physical gesture going on, which makes all the difference.'

Learning to use the voice effectively involves singing as well as speaking. Although there was a piano in the upper room at Queen Charlotte Street, singing was not a major part of the training until Duncan Ross employed a teacher of 'Voice Production with a view to Singing', German-trained opera-singer Nell Moody, who had helped him to get over a lung operation when he was a young actor at the Old Vic: 'I taught voice production from basic poise - about which I learnt a tremendous amount myself from Rudi,' says Mrs Moody. 'I taught very much from the fact that, ten to one, if you stand right, your breathing is natural. I was very against forcing young voices. You should never divorce the ability to make a pleasant singing sound from your own speaking voice. In those days we had nothing in the way of music in the School. Some of them knew something about Gilbert and Sullivan, some of them knew pop, so we started with that, but after about two years we had *The Marriage of Figaro* and little duets from *La Traviata* and the hits of the time, things like *South Pacific*. Rudi was responsible for movement and dancing, and I enjoyed working with him enormously, because we did more and more a combination of natural physical movement with the making of sound.'

Mrs Moody had come to Bristol in 1954 (when her husband John, who had been for five years Director of the new Arts Council, was appointed Director of the Bristol Old Vic) and taught singing at the Theatre School until December 1960. The Moodys became, according to John's 1993 obituary in *Opera* magazine, 'the best of surrogate parents to a generation of would-be Hamlets and Violettas, their house in Bristol alive with energy and helpful determination'. Gene Wilder left the BOV Theatre School in 1956 without completing the course, but was, he writes, 'nevertheless grateful for some of the classes in physical techniques ... In particular, I remember one magnificent teacher, Mrs Moody, who taught singing. It was the most beneficial class I had.'

Many have equally positive memories of Nell Moody's successor, Bristolian John Oxley, who joined the School in January 1961, having studied at the Royal College of Music and worked as a singer in the West End and on tour. He established Singing as part of the full time curriculum, with groups of five or six instead of the previously established fifteen-minute individual lesson for which students left other classes.

Students describe John Oxley as a straightforward, avuncular and jovial man, and have a special fondness for his favoured training song, *Ombra Mai Fu*. He had an impressive way of demonstrating the power of the breath: 'He would get you to put your arms around his chest and hold as tight as you could, then he would breathe in and always break the hold with the power of his lungs.' And he taught actors to focus their breath in such a way that their voice would come out from the top of the head, because even humming quietly can then be heard right up in the 'Gods' of a theatre.

John Oxley claimed to be able to teach anyone to sing, no matter how unpromising they seemed when they arrived. He used to give a special Saturday class for people who had a 'faulty ear', affecting not only their singing but also the range of their speaking voice, and their ability to vary its pitch: 'At the end of a year, I would have them singing unaccompanied in two parts,' he says with pride. 'He worked wonders with the "tone-deaf" group,' writes Heida Steindors. 'Their concerts are unforgettable!'

'He showed me that in order to act, you didn't need to put on a special voice. An acting voice is simply an extension of your ordinary voice, and a singing voice is simply another extension of that,' says Christopher Ashley. 'I remember trying to sing and John pushing me around, punching me and shaking me, all the time I was trying to sing he was pushing me on the floor and rolling me around - to try and lose some of the stiffness I had. So many of us were so rigid as students.'

When John Oxley left in the summer of 1975, Rita McKerrow returned to the Theatre School, where she has taught singing ever since. Rita had been one of the first BOVTS students in 1946, taking evening classes because she was often away in London, working on broadcasts and concerts. Her ambition was to be an opera singer, and to go to Glyndebourne, which she did for the first of eight seasons in 1949, the start of a long career as a professional singer and teacher.

Rita's canine companions have proved unforgettable. Many students have particularly vivid memories of Muzzeltot ('Muzzli'), a sort of Jack Russell that usually sat in a basket in a corner of the music room, often howling along with the singing practice, and occasionally working itself into a frenzy on everyone's legs (or the piano if all else failed). Others recall that Rita wasn't tall enough to see over the top of the piano, which they took as a licence to play the fool. She had her own ways of making the lessons enjoyable, using funny singing exercises which she had learned from various professionals.

In the first year, Rita McKerrow and, since 1995,

professional singer Pamela Rudge, teach the basics of technique, then in the second year Neil Rhoden coaches students in singing: 'It's not just about getting the notes right, it's about how you present a number. It's a combination of musical and acting talents: a singer has to put across whatever the song is about, to make sense of the lyrics so that what you say in a song is just as meaningful and real as if they'd been speaking rather than singing,' says Neil, who was Musical Director on the first British tours of *Company* and *A Little Night Music,* on *Side By Side By Sondheim* in the West End, and on all the BOV Company's musical productions from autumn 1969 until the early 1980s.

'With a student who has never done any singing before, you start with the ear, trying to make people notice differences in pitch,' says Neil, who first worked for BOVTS on the 1981 production of *Joseph and the Amazing Technicolor Dreamcoat* at the Hippodrome, and joined the full time staff in 1983. 'That's important to acting as well as singing: whether you lift an inflection or let it fall matters to the sense and subtext of what you're saying. With music, it's very precise: they're given a note and they have to be able to sing it back. Then they have to understand rhythm. And we like them to be able to read music by the time they leave here, so that if ever music is thrown at them they can go home, play it out on a piano or a recorder and be able to learn it overnight and go back to an audition able to sing it. Some can leave with a couple of hundred songs that they could stand up and sing for an audition; the less gifted will have at least ten or twelve that they can do well, and will be able to learn new songs, given a little more time.'

Nat Brenner always said that anyone who works in the theatre needs to be musical, not necessarily to sing and dance, but to be able to listen accurately and to have a precise sense of timing: 'He was a master of farce, explaining that it only works when the performance has a musical kind of rhythm.'

'Some people arrive here with three left feet and unable to sing a note in tune!' Neil Rhoden smiles. 'They never leave here like that. That doesn't mean they're ever going to earn their living out of dancing and singing. It's actually about making an actor. As an actor, your voice and your body are your only tools, and singing and dancing are among the best technically accomplished ways of training them: controlled, disciplined movement and noise-making.'

Understanding music is also important for Technical students, some of whom go on to work for ballet and opera companies: Neil's second-in-command, Andrew Allpass, often works as a musician for the BOV Company, and plays for auditions at the School as well as teaching the Technical students what a musical score looks like, how to read it, and what it means; Tim Williams, who trained at BOVTS as both an actor and a stage manager, regularly returns to the School to give practice and advice in cueing from music. Tim is now one of the top commercial Company Managers in live theatre and ballet - and one of the few stage managers who can cue the popular but notoriously difficult *Three Dances for Japanese Music,* which uses a tape of the Kodo Drummers and no written score at all.

26. Christopher Denys, Principal of the Bristol Old Vic Theatre School since 1980, directing a production of David Wood's *Meg and Mog Show* at the Redgrave Theatre.

27. BOVTS in *The Mysteries,* adapted from the Wakefield, York and Chester Cycles by Christopher Denys (New Vic, spring 1981).

28. *Salad Days* originals: Bob Harris (Troppo) and Minnie (piano).

29. BOVTS in the 30th anniversary production of *Salad Days* in 1984, the first revival in the Theatre Royal since 1954.

30. BOVTS in Agatha Christie's *Spider's Web* (Little Theatre, November 1986).

31. BOVTS in *The Beggar's Opera* by John Gay (West Country Tour 1988).

32. BOVTS in *Company* by Stephen Sondheim (Theatre Royal, June 1992).

33. BOVTS in *The Nativity*, adapted by Christopher Denys (December 1992).

34. BOVTS in *Alice in Wonderland* by Lewis Carroll, adapted by
Christopher Denys and Neil Rhoden (Redgrave Theatre, December 1993).

35. BOVTS in *The Jungle
Book* by Rudyard Kipling,
adapted by John Hartoch
(West Country Tour 1994
and Swan Theatre,
Stratford-upon-Avon 1995).

36. BOVTS in *Hiawatha* by Henry Longfellow, adapted by Francis Thomas (T-I-E tour, February 1995).

37. BOVTS in *Red Noses* by Peter Barnes (New Vic, June 1995).

38. Students at work in the Slade/Reynolds Studio, built in 1995 and named after the co-writers of *Salad Days.*

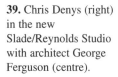

39. Chris Denys (right)
in the new
Slade/Reynolds Studio
with architect George
Ferguson (centre).

40. and **41**. The Bristol Old Vic Theatre School in 1996.

16. Behind the scenes: let's get technical

It was only after Nat Brenner arrived at the Theatre Royal in 1950 that the School advertised separate courses for Technical students. Bob Harris was one of the first: 'The first term, we were expected to do the same course as the actors. The other two terms, we were used in the Theatre, and were divorced from the School really. It was not unlike other sorts of apprenticeship in those days, where you paid to learn your profession,' recalls Bob, who was taken on as an ASM at the Theatre Royal after training, staying until 1954, when he went to London with *Salad Days,* in which he played the original Troppo for seven years.

When the Theatre School moved to Downside Road, the space used by Technical students was spread about the buildings, encouraging an unusually intimate relationship between Acting and non-Acting courses: there were wardrobe and prop making studios on the top floor of 1 Downside Road, a lecture studio on the second floor, and 'incredibly cramped' scenery workshops in the basement, 'with a floor encrusted with glue and paint, and a reek of size and resin'. Leading the Technical courses at BOVTS in the late 1950s, Michael Ackland carried on the tradition of the London Old Vic Theatre School, which he describes as 'not just a place where one studied acting, design, painting, model-making, and suchlike but a dynamic, integrated theatrical experience where one was expected to gain an understanding of style, acting, management and production even if one was not going to become an actor, manager or producer.'

Each autumn would start with a new group of twelve students - four designers, up to half a dozen stage managers or technicians, and between two and four who wanted to learn about everything. Looking back, Michael Ackland sees that 'To pack into a year all the technical and mundane details of stagecraft together with an intensive study of style could sometimes be counterproductive,' and he had quite a job persuading Duncan Ross not to start massive productions in the first term, which was the beginning of the second year of the Acting course. Despite the practical problem of having to give Technical students a grounding in the basics at the same time as the actors were impatient to get on the stage, the Technical courses remained one year until the early 1980s.

By 1957, Ross had introduced a three year 'sandwich course', which stayed in the prospectus until 1969, offering two years of Acting, with a middle of year on the Technical course: having applied for this course, Althea Stewart actually did the two year Acting course, then combined further acting with a final year as a Technical student. When Althea found her career as an actress and stage manager curtailed by having three young children, she became Recording Editor at Calibre Cassette Library for the Handicapped, where, she writes, 'the technical and administrative skills that I learned from Michael Ackland were invaluable, and Duncan Ross's advice about looking for the right sound for key words often made it easier to record a complex passage in a book.'

It was always possible for students at BOVTS to adapt their studies to their aptitudes: 'One of my finest students, a fellow called John Toogood, was originally on the acting course,' recalled Roger Jeffery in 1994. 'He came to the conclusion himself after one year that he was a lousy actor and said "I'll make myself a good stage manager". And my golly, he did more than that. He became a very highly respected Production Manager, doing all the big West End stuff, and then General Manager of the Prince Edward Theatre.' For some it worked the other way round: among those who originally trained as stage managers and later became performers are Ian Bolt, Abigail McKern, and Michael Sharvell-Martin, who started in rep 'as ASM, Stage Manager, Company Manager, electrician and all sorts, eventually changing over to acting after about five years, which I have been doing successfully ever since'.

Roger Jeffery was Technical Director at BOVTS from 1961 to 1983, and worked with one full time assistant (usually an ex-student) plus a selection of visiting tutors from the Company, the University, and the West of England College of Art. After a diploma course in Drama as an actor/teacher, and two years' National Service, his first job in 1954 had been as an ASM 'on a pantomime with the mighty Stoll Theatre Corporation, earning £5 a week, which seemed quite reasonable at the time. It was four shillings more than I was paid in the RAF!' He went on to work in the West End and touring, mainly on musicals (including the smash hit of the day, *The Pajama Game*) before setting up a small stage lighting company, which brought him into regular contact with the Bristol Old Vic Theatre School and Company. He became Technical Director of the Theatre School while Duncan Ross was the Principal, and stayed for twenty-two years, seventeen of them with Nat Brenner. After leaving BOVTS, Roger worked for five years in corporate video training and as a commercial conference director until a rare degenerative disease forced him to retire, though he continued his active involvement with the Backwell Playhouse and training young theatre people right up to his death, aged 61, in April 1996.

Roger also chose a dozen students each year, covering a cross-section of skills and interests that would service all aspects of the School's productions: 'I was mainly looking for people who wanted to learn, and for some evidence of intelligent life!' Vivienne Cozens, who became a television director, remembers having to go to the School and do 'an extraordinarily intricate test - solving puzzles, which I suppose was to see if we were practically minded'. Fellow-student Marcia Wheeler, later a BBC Drama Producer and Training Manager, remembers their ingenious solutions to the lack of convenient refreshments at Downside Road and the University Drama Studio: they 'built a mobile canteen, shaped something like a coffin, with brass knobs at the corners, a drop down front and a wheeled base which could be towed behind a bicycle. We charged the Acting students two or three pence for tea or coffee - but they had to provide their own clean cups ... When we did overnight set-ups in the Studio we had a very old hotplate which took twenty minutes to boil a kettle, so it had its own cue on the lighting board so that tea could be ready in time for the interval!'

Everyone was encouraged to learn all the basics of theatre life regardless of where they eventually wanted to specialise: 'You learnt from doing it - which is how people used to learn when they went straight into the job. We had a different job on every show, and it was hands-on all the way through,' says Carol A Smith.

'But we weren't actually allowed to *do* anything for the first six weeks,' adds Wayne Dowdeswell, the RSC's Stratford-based lighting wizard, who has been Chief at The Swan Theatre since it opened in 1986. 'We sat in a classroom and were given lectures and demonstrations, which we found rather frustrating, but it did give us the grounding to do the job reliably and safely when we were finally released on productions.'

Looking back to the 1960s and 1970s, when Nat Brenner presented as many as four shows in repertoire at the Theatre Royal, Roger Jeffery recalled being 'confronted with the logistical problem of how to get these shows on and off the stage. And we're not talking about slightly staged productions. We had to get one full production off stage and the new one on, very often in the space of forty-five minutes, which was the time available between curtain down on the matinée and curtain up on the evening show. I was later told by an ex-student that people used to say "If you got through a year with Roger Jeffery on the Bristol Old Vic Tech course, you can work anywhere" and I took that as a sort of backhanded compliment.'

After introducing the first three year Acting course in 1969, Nat Brenner reorganised the Technical courses in 1970, when the School began to offer the possibility of a second year for up to half a dozen Stage Management students, mainly those who hoped to become designers or directors. Numbers gradually increased from twelve up to fifteen, and eventually twenty, making it possible for Roger Jeffery to widen the scope of the training: 'I believe I was one of the first in the country to initiate student attachments - what they now call "work experience" - to theatre companies or associated businesses, sending them off for two weeks or a month as an extra unpaid assistant, which was a marvellous chance to learn by observing the professionals.'

Many of the students were regularly employed - alongside Roger himself - as show staff on pantomimes and touring shows at the Bristol Hippodrome: 'I can vividly remember the night I was working on *The Black and White Minstrels* and the tape to which the company and the show orchestra mimed broke down! The stand by tape, which ran in synch with the main show tape also failed, and the show literally ground to a halt,' says Chris Smith, whose career as a techie took him from the theatre to television, radio, and rock 'n' roll, before he became a writer and public relations man. The standard course was extended to two years in autumn 1981, when the number of students doubled to forty, twenty in each year. Cliff Zenker, who joined BOVTS as Production Manager in 1982 and was Head of Technical Courses from 1983 to 1985, consolidated the changeover from a one year course and began the process of making the training much more structured, with the benefit of his own recent experience in the profession. After training at Central School of Speech and Drama, he had worked his way up from ASM to DSM at Salisbury, then joined the BOV Company as a Deputy Stage Manager in 1978, been Company Manager in both the New Vic and the Theatre Royal, and freelanced in the world of London conferences and corporate tours.

Paul Rummer has been Head of Technical Courses since 1985 and an Associate Principal since 1989: 'It never occurred to me to train - I didn't know you could! I started working when it was still the norm to progress through from casual work and learn on the job. That doesn't happen now, mainly because most Production Managers have had drama school training and know the advantages that it brings. But even then the BOV / BOVTS network was so vast and influential that I seem to have done a sort of Bristol Old Vic 'distance learning' course! When I finished a French Literature degree at Sussex University - having spent most of my time doing casual work in the local theatre - I found work as a technician at Warwick Arts Centre, where I met Bristol people. At the Gardner Arts Centre in Brighton the Administrator was Nigel Stannard (ex BOV Tour Manager), the Production Manager was Peter Bailey (ex BOV and BOVTS), guest Directors included John David (ex BOVTS, and BOV Artistic Director) and the Master Carpenter was Alf Gleason (ex BOV Master Carpenter). Then at Chichester Festival Theatre the Stage Manager was Pip Royall (ex BOV Stage Management) and it went on from there.'

The early 1990s' expansion of higher education made it possible for drama schools to offer degree courses, but, says Paul Rummer, 'We still firmly believe ours should remain a two year practical course, keeping abreast of new developments'.

There has been a paper qualification at the end of the course - a BTEC Higher National Diploma in Performing Arts (Stage Management) - since 1994. But in practice the students do much the same work as before, with a more formal assessment procedure based on five basic 'modules': stage management, carpentry, prop making, lighting, and sound. There's also a sort of multi-skilling sixth module covering technical drawing, welding, video, radio, voice, photography, publicity, administration, first aid, production management, history of theatre, and playreadings.

In many ways, stage management depends on what people call 'common sense' - which is not as common as it sounds. The key word is communication: 'You're the one in the middle making things run smoothly for the actors, the director, the technicians and the audience. You need to be a good organiser, of both people and paper, very practical, and very patient. And a sense of humour is an absolute must - without that you would go round the bend.'

The teaching at BOVTS has always been based on what happens in a repertory theatre, reflecting the job most students do when they leave, but it's readily adapted to every other working situation they're likely to meet: 'You had a go at everything, so you understand what everyone else's jobs are - which is part of your job as a stage manager, to know how everything works and to make sure things are going how they should. You're dealing with very highly skilled people - on the stage crew, in the wardrobe, electricians, welders - and you really have to know your stuff for them to respect you,' says Annie McGann, who now uses her stage management skills to organise large-scale 'rave' events, and her prop-making talents to create 'chill-out room' interactive environments. 'The health and safety inspections are very strict, but the new regulations are not really new to someone who's worked in theatre. I can instinctively tell if something is punter-proof, because I've had so much experience of making sure things are actor-proof!'

Dawn Monaghan and Cyril Gates work together for BBC Manchester: 'Although we were at the Theatre School at different times, we knew lots of the same teachers and find a lot of what we do in our everyday working life has been moulded by it,' says Dawn, whose coursework in quarter-inch tape editing and floor managing helped to get her a first job with the BBC after leaving BOVTS. 'I get very frustrated with colleagues who haven't got a sense of urgency, or who rush into a job so fast that they never see the hurdle and they fall down the hole. If there's one thing that Bristol Old Vic taught me, it's to stand back and say "What could possibly go wrong?" and then make sure that it doesn't. That's the art of good stage management, and it works every time.'

Once they've grasped the basics of what stage management involves, from setting up a company through to running a show, the students make their own 'prompt book' - the all-important copy of the script that contains a detailed record of the particular production: entrances and exits; cuts and cues; props, people and practically everything else that the director, designer, actors and technicians have worked out during the preparation and rehearsals. The prompt book has to be clear and easy to follow - it's referred to as 'a sort of Bible' and whoever is 'on the book' during a show has complete control. But it can also be lively and colourful, with patches of material stuck on sketches of the costumes, outlines of the stage and set design (of which the students also make three-dimensional models) and mysterious-looking codes that will translate into changing patterns of light and sound.

Meanwhile, down in the basement, Technical Stage Manager Brian Buttle has been in charge of the workshop since 1988, following in the tradition of previous Master Carpenters Frank Fresko, James Woodard, Terry Round and Bob Redman: 'Being able to understand and interpret technical drawings is very important, because the set-builders have to read the designer's plans and make them into a three-dimensional reality,' says Brian, who originally came to BOVTS as a mature student in 1982, for one year of the Stage Management course and a second on the Directors' Attachment. 'The whole basis of everything we do in the theatre is paperwork. If you get the paperwork right, the rest is pure joy.'

All the students do a carpentry project in the second term, making anything from small cabinets and tables to tool boxes or bookshelves. They learn enough about different kinds of wood cuts and joints to be useful DIY enthusiasts, though 'it's a different approach at home than on the stage,' explains

BOVTS-trained Carol Mackenzie, who freelances as a carpenter and teaches part time at the Theatre School. 'In the theatre, you know that you're building *not* to last, so you make do with glue and banging in the odd nail instead of making proper joints because it's all going to be pulled apart in a few weeks' time.'

'A lot of progress can be made when you break rules, but you have to learn the rules first, and understand their value - then only break them if there's a good reason to,' adds Brian, who can often be heard telling students 'It's the glue that does the work' or 'Measure twice and cut once', and who also teaches the techniques of old-fashioned stagecraft. He shows students how to canvas a flat properly, and how to throw a 'cleat', which is two hooks with a rope designed to fit two stage flats together quickly. Depending on the shows and the timetable, students may also have a chance to learn 'flying' at the Theatre Royal - the process of raising and lowering scenery (and sometimes people - like Peter Pan!) with a precise and intricate set of counterweighted pulleys and tied-off ropes. 1995 graduate Rob Sayer had already 'flown' before he came to the School, and did his work placement with a specialist firm called Unusual Rigging, helping to fit up the massive VE Day Celebrations in Hyde Park.

What is now the Quiet Room on the first floor of 1 Downside Road was once the domain of Liz Fjelle when she was in charge of prop making at BOVTS, from the late 1970s until 1989. Liz had been a Design student at the School, had her own props shop in Lower Redland Road, and was constantly involved in a wide range of local design projects - from Chris Harris's professional solo show *Ally Sloper's Half Holiday* to a large-scale Bristol community play at St James Barton Church: 'Liz was a superbly talented creative artist, and more a sculptural than a painterly sort of designer,' according to Roger Jeffery. 'She had the most enormous gnarled hands, with clay under her fingernails, knitting needles in her hair, and bits of fibreglass sticking to her everywhere. And she produced the most beautiful props out of the most unlikely cheap materials: I believe she could have made a silk purse out of a sow's ear.'

Liz Fjelle was the Props Mistress when David Rigden, who took over as Props Master, was a Stage Management student at BOVTS: 'I intended to be a stage manager, and it was an added advantage that the School covers lighting and sound and props and carpentry so well,' says David, who had already worked as a carpenter and prop maker in amateur theatre and on a community programme. 'The more you put into the course, the more you get out of it, and the more strings you have to your bow when you go out into the profession.' David went out as an ASM in rep, and while working as a DSM at Northampton expanded into making props for a pantomime, 'which was great fun - the highlight of the year, creating larger than life stuff like foam rubber hammers, huge baby's bottles and an oversized dentist's drill.' When he first returned to Bristol, he combined freelancing as a prop maker with teaching part time at the School, where he is now based full time in a small office and two basement workshops (one of them part of the old Movement Studio) where he demonstrates all the possible materials and modelling techniques necessary for students to produce anything from a realistic severed hand to a full-scale mock-up of an Edwardian vintage car.

Lighting and sound technology has developed beyond the dreams of science fiction from those early days just after the war when the Bristol Old Vic Company lit the Theatre Royal stage with one of Frederick Bentham's Strand Lighting Consoles (in which the previous switches, levers and shafting of a lighting board had been replaced by the keys and stopkeys of what looked like a cinema organ) and played its sound effects on a panatrope ('pan' for short, a twin turntable using 78rpm discs). The Stage Manager had to mark out the relevant passages with a short pencil and put the needle down in exactly the right place at exactly the right moment, which was terrifyingly difficult. Even when Chris Denys was an Associate Director with the BOV Company in the early 1960s, 'they were still using the panatrope, plus one Series 4 Ferrograph - and I added a home-made mixer.'

In the 1990s, sound effects in the Theatre Royal are operated with a combination of digital samplers and recordable optical discs which are triggered directly from a keyboard that can operate up to a hundred and twenty different effects - all hiss-free, crackle-free, and much more convenient: 'The days of the poor old tape recorder have been numbered since the arrival of compact discs and digital technology. Theatres are investing in the new equipment because of the quality and freedom that digital sound can now offer,' says John Waterhouse, who joined the Theatre School staff in 1984 as Head of Lighting and Sound, which has evolved to include responsibility for the School's computer resources and link to the Internet. In the autumn of 1995, the Bristol Old Vic Theatre School was the first British drama school to publish its prospectus on the Net, which it uses to market the School as well as for gleaning information and new contacts within the many related industries worldwide.

John Waterhouse studied sciences at Bath Tech, and started in the industry by helping out with a local folk group, learning about sound balancing, sound engineering and PA ('Public Address') systems as he went along. Experience in touring, TV, radio and recording studios eventually landed him a job at the Welsh National Opera on the strength of his reputation and contacts: 'The early seventies were a time of "*who* you knew" rather than "*what* you knew" when it came to finding work in the entertainment industry. But the latter part of the seventies saw some wonderful leaps in theatre techniques and technology, and by the time I was in a position to recruit staff myself, it was really necessary for them to have relevant training before they would even be considered.'

John worked with the WNO for ten years, not only on sound but also extensively with lighting, becoming Chief Electrician and resident Lighting Designer in 1977: 'I learnt more about the art of stage lighting by working with talented directors than I ever learnt by reading technical books or even working alongside fellow lighting designers. John Moody, who'd been at Bristol Old Vic in the 1950s, had been joint Artistic Director at the Welsh National since 1970. He taught me so much in my earlier years about the importance of precision within lighting and often hounded me when we were out on tour by sending reams of notes about the tiniest of lighting details, complete with attached hieroglyphics of lighting spot adjustments drawn perfectly to scale on graph paper. He could still perceive a misplaced spotlight that was only four inches off its target at the age of seventy from the back of the "Gods" at the New Theatre Cardiff!'

To allow John Waterhouse to spend more time on computers and new technology, the School recruited another of its graduates to teach the basics of lighting and sound, to help on video projects and Stage Management classes, and to supervise productions. Ruth Sidery worked in stage management for regional theatres and small scale touring companies, then for over two years at Taunton's Brewhouse Theatre where she could also use her technical skills. She returned to Bristol Old Vic in 1995 as Stage Manager for a Theatre Royal production, before joining the School's staff.

Students have access to a broad range of equipment dating from 1956 to the present, and although the School can't always afford to buy the latest and most expensive items, it does keep in line with what is representative in the business: 'Not all of our equipment is exactly what the industry uses, yet students can learn the techniques here because the principles and methods of working are the same,' says John Waterhouse. 'The hardest part of teaching audio is how to give students a visual picture of how sound actually moves through the equipment - I used to explain it in terms of "little men" travelling through underground mazes - until someone accused me of being sexist. Now I talk about "little people"!'

Over the years John has learned not to force the technology on the students too early: 'I try to teach lighting and sound with a sense of fun, otherwise people who only want to become stage managers tend to glaze over. For their first technical lecture we take them to Bristol's hands-on science centre, The Exploratory, which is a wonderful adventure for everybody.' A certain amount of chalk and blackboard teaching is essential, but John lightens up the theory classes 'with videos on animation or radio production, maybe a few tricks with colour that show them how easily their eyes and mind can be confused, or even a customised computer game that allows them to role play a Stage Manager!'

In the 1940s, when directors also designed the lighting, Hugh Hunt would demonstrate to BOVTS students how he lit his productions: all the plans were done on graph paper, with a circle to show if a light was from above, or an elliptical drawing if it was from the side. Computers have made a big difference: there have been computer memory desks since the early 1970s - when lighting design began to be recognised as a separate specialist skill: 'Nowadays computer technology allows you to achieve tremendous efficiency and control of all facets of stage lighting,' says John Waterhouse, 'but only if you have a very generous budget, which is why digitally controlled robotic spotlights are still more prominent in commercial presentations and TV than in regional theatres.'

After mastering all the basic essentials in the classroom, the first years do practical exercises within their own group, using short scripts which they have to put on the stage, building the set, recording the sound, rigging the lights, doing all the cueing and prompting - and even acting the parts. They start with specially-written one-act plays like *The Haunted House,* which crams lots of obvious props and simple cues into only three pages of script, and work up to complicated scenarios like those in Alan Ayckbourn's farcical *Gosforth's Fete,* or Victoria Wood's spoof soap opera *Acorn Antiques.* So that the students can see how well they've done, these performances are recorded on video by BOVTS Chief Electrician Gerry Douglas, who joined the School in 1986 as a Technical Assistant.

'Each exercise gets a bit more complex and a bit longer,' explains Carol A Smith, who had come back to BOVTS in 1981 as a Stage Management Tutor, and went on to become Deputy Head of the Technical Course and Course Administrator. 'In the second term we add video, and they shadow the second years tech-ing the lunchtime shows; in the third term, when the actors' lunchtime plays are repeated, they take on full responsibility for tech-ing them, while working as crew on the School's main shows in the Theatre Royal and New Vic.'

In their second year, much of the students' time is taken up by responsibility for providing set, props, lighting, sound and stage management for all the School's public stage shows, sharing the jobs so that everyone tries their hand at everything, helped out by first years on the fit-ups and get-outs. The School doesn't have its own theatre, and there is very little space at Downside Road to do practical lighting work, but BOVTS makes a virtue out of a necessity by using local theatres like the New Vic and Clifton College's Redgrave for teaching, helping to make students more adaptable by giving them experience of different environments, equipment and technical staffs.

Stage Management as well as Acting students have always had opportunities to work with the Company on fit-ups and get-outs, but there are now fewer opportunities to work on professional productions, as Paul Rummer explains: 'When I was a Stage Manager for the BOV Company in the early 1980s, I inherited a system of using Technical students from the School when we needed casual workers in the Studio, but it's been much more difficult since the early 1990s, because the New Vic has been closed for part of the time, and has since hosted more and more small-scale touring productions and less of the Company's own work. We still use the Studio for our own productions, and for teaching, and it's a wonderful place to get experience because it's a user-friendly size where the stage managers can get involved in rigging lights and operating sound as well as the organisational side of the job. In the Theatre Royal, the scale is so much bigger that the work has to be much more demarcated, and is usually done by the specialist departments.'

During the second year, students spend three weeks on 'work experience' attachment to a professional company where they can develop their particular interests: some in theatres; others in scenery workshops, or television or recording studios. The etiquette of floor managing in TV or video is very similar to stage management in theatre, and those who are interested learn enough at BOVTS to get them off on a good footing with an independent video company or as a runner with the BBC.

Since the early 1990s, video has also been put to an ingenious use for training first year stage managers, using recordings of School productions: 'We use these as a sort of "poor man's interactive video",' explains John Waterhouse. 'We take the video and a large TV monitor into the actual theatre where we have recorded the previous night's performance. First year stage management, lighting and sound students then attempt to run the performance by listening just to the recorded voices of the actors in the control box. If the students succeed, then we get a perfect performance of technical operations without a real actor in sight. Everything that should be seen and heard on the real stage is confirmed by the video.'

What the students don't hear is an extra separate soundtrack on which all the communications between the second year stage managers during the live performance were recorded, allowing the tutors to compare what the first year students do with what the real operators did: 'The nice thing is that if we make a mistake, we just rewind the tape - which is very much like what happens in a real technical rehearsal in the theatre,' says John, who looks forward to a time when all this can be done on a computer, or even in virtual reality!

Actual reality has seen Technical students from BOVTS go into a remarkably wide range of careers, though most make a start as Assistant Stage Managers in live theatre: 'Our Bristol education meant we could do things like change a plug, understand a plan, screw, nail, wiggle-pin and glue anything together; organise, motivate, build a team. It taught you to listen, to be heard, to finish what you started or, if you couldn't, to find some other mug that could (or, as it's politely called, to delegate),' writes Maggie Bosworth. 'I did a lot of temping work in the holidays and I was offered every job I did at the end of my time, mainly because in the theatre whatever you did, however bad or stupid, you had to admit to your mistake because you realised that the knock-on effect would be tragic (no-one had ever known a temp do that!).'

Peter Bailey, who was the first ASM in the BOV's New Vic in 1972, Company Stage Manager in the Theatre Royal from 1975-78 and Production Manager from 1980-86, teamed up with BOV / BOVTS carpenter Bob Redman in 1985 to form a successful Bristol-based company of scenery manufacturers, providing local employment for many more BOVTS students. Luke Sapsed started working as a stage hand at the Theatre Royal while still a student, was taken on by the BOV Company as a Lighting Assistant, and went on to be Promotions Manager at London's Canary Wharf until spring 1996, when he became Director of Bristol's Watershed Media Centre. Julian Courtenay had his first job with the BOV Company as an ASM, and progressed to being General Manager of London's Savoy Theatre.

After training at the BOV Theatre School and working with the Company, John Leonard has become one of the most highly respected Sound men in the business, and the only technician ever to become an Associate Member of the RSC. Lorraine Laybourne joined the BOV Company as an Assistant Technician in 1987 and has been Deputy Chief Electrician since 1990. Claire Mason stage managed in rep for ten years, and had jobs ranging from touring an Australian folk band around the Outback to being 'on the book' for five hundred performances of *The Mousetrap* before joining the stage management accreditation panel of the National Council for Drama Training - returning, like NCDT panel-member Marcia Wheeler, to assess the Bristol courses. After stage managing in rep and at the RSC, Ian G James took an Arts Administration course at the City Lit, later spending three years as Administrator with innovative dance troupes The Cholmondeleys and The Featherstonehaughs.

'My training at the BOVTS has enabled me to have two careers,' writes Dr Jeffrey Grenfell-Hill, who became Director of Sixth Form Studies at a school in Harpenden. 'I also adjudicate at the leading speech and drama festivals, and travel all over the UK as a senior examiner for LAMDA.' Rachel Niblock became Head of Stage Management at Oxford School of Drama in 1994 after working as a stage manager in regional theatre and the West End, and as a freelance prop maker and buyer. The talents Nikki Skinner developed at BOVTS proved useful in jobs ranging from making props and setting scenes as a shop window dresser to Production Manager for a publisher of theatre programmes. As well as lighting large scale festivals for the Italian city of Bologna and 'objects, casts of one to two hundred and forty, back rooms of pubs, and main stages, indoors and out,' Chahine Yavroyan has worked as a performer, sound designer and production manager with dozens of companies, including 'People Shows Number 85 to 100 and still counting...'

Stage Management and Technical training at the Theatre School can give you a sort of Access All Areas pass to working on commercial trade presentations: 'Some of the people who work regularly in conferencing are ex-students from Bristol,' says Cliff Zenker, naming 'Tristian Bickerton, who works for Delta Sound; Andy Clarke, who's a freelance video technician; Daniel Nissel, who worked for production company MWA; and Emma Bingham, who's a stage manager/show caller.' When Cliff introduced teaching sessions on trade and conference productions in the mid-1980s, he impressed on students who wanted to work in that area that they would benefit from having professional theatre experience because the work is so similar: 'What our clients call "meetings", we still refer to as "shows". They need show callers - people on the book; they need stage management, budget control and production management; and they need a high degree of technical knowledge. People who've trained in the theatre understand the way the shows work. If you've been a DSM on the book for a large panto, then you'll have no problem running one of the big car shows, or spectacular "reveals".'

The technical and management skills used on the stage are equally relevant in theme parks and leisure centres such as Alton Towers, Somerwest World and Legoland, all of which have included BOVTS graduates on their staff. Paul Neville's first job after leaving BOVTS was as Technical Manager of the 1986 National Garden Festival in Stoke, 'running an entertainments programme which included a big arena where the American Civil War Society did their thing, JCB did its "dancing diggers" show, and we had everything from professional bands to jugglers and kiddies dancing.'

Mike Ostler, who later became Vice Chairman and Publicity Officer for the Society for Theatre Research, returned to Bristol as a film projectionist, was Box Office Manager for the BOV Company at the Little Theatre in the early 1970s, and in 1996 manages a multiplex cinema in Grays, Essex.

'The technical course at the Theatre School didn't specifically cover film projection, but it was a good grounding to learn any new technical skill, because it's always a matter of logic and attention to detail - and checking, checking, and checking again,' says Clare England, who in 1994 became Deputy Technician and Projectionist at Bristol's Arnolfini, where BOVTS-trained Terry Sheppard had been Chief Technician in the 1980s.

Jackie Vance, daughter of theatre producer Charles Vance, went into film editing; Alex Cox started in theatre then moved into television as a freelance production manager and location manager; and Sam Breckman is a top location manager for the BBC, with the major TV drama series based on Jane Austen's *Pride and Prejudice* and George Eliot's *Middlemarch* among his 1990s' credits.

Joe Aveline has worked in the entertainment industry ever since taking the BOVTS technical course in 1959-60: 'I am currently a Council Member of the Association of British Theatre Technicians, as well as on the Executive of the

International Organisation of Scenographers, Theatre Architects and Technicians (OISTAT) with members in 37 countries worldwide. I have also contributed a section to the book *Effects for the Theatre,* published in July 1995 by A&C Black. I mention these things because, to this day, I feel certain that the BOVTS provided me with a springboard to make a lot of these things happen.'

17. By design: creating sets and costumes

'Design can be anything from a chair and a pair of swimming trunks to a huge helicopter which is flown in while soldiers in full uniform are doing battle in the background,' explains one Design student at BOVTS, where a separate one-year postgraduate course was set up in 1970, replacing an arrangement whereby designers had been an integral part of the general Technical course. It's a hands-on, intensive practical experience, in which people learn how to apply their previous artistic skills and knowledge to the special demands of the theatre, where they will need to communicate clearly with carpenters and prop makers as well as stage managers and directors, and to have a basic understanding of all kinds of construction and decoration. At BOVTS, they have the added advantage of being able to design for productions that will actually be staged in the Bristol Old Vic's historic Theatre Royal and modern New Vic studio as well as for shows in local theatres like Bristol's Redgrave and small-scale touring to schools, church halls and community arts centres.

In the mid-1950s there were few avenues to learning theatre design in Britain: there were no degree courses in fine arts until the 1960s, and art college training tended to be theoretical rather than practical; few theatre schools offered any kind of technical training, and BOVTS was the only one attached to a working theatre. Before training at Bristol in 1956, Fluff Browne (now Catherine Hayes-Davies) already had a National Diploma in Theatre Design from Wimbledon Art School, where the students' only contact with the real theatre was seeing London productions on spare evenings! The Theatre School clearly went several stages further: 'The first year actors and the techs spent the first term learning about the workings of a production by class work. We joined the Acting students for some of the classes and were not allowed to be spectators all the time. I remember George Brandt teaching me to hit the mat really hard in Judo and Rudi Shelly pinning trains on us to teach us period movement,' she recalls, further illustrating the holistic attitude of Duncan Ross, who expected all students to have just as rounded an appreciation of theatre whether they were going to work on the stage or behind it. Presented with a prompt copy of Chekhov's *The Seagull,* all the students were expected to research for the 'gone before' (what had occurred to bring the characters to their present condition), then designers and stage managers were asked to make a logical ground plan of the house and gardens while the actors set about discovering the characters through improvisation.

Although most of its own productions were presented in the University Drama Studio, Technical students were sent down to the Theatre Royal every third weekend to work on the get-out of one show and the fit-up for the next. Thus Catherine Hayes-Davies was already familiar with the Theatre Royal when she began her professional career there, officially as Property Mistress though one of her first tasks was to design John Moody's production of *Under Milk Wood!* After a three-year interval working as an Assistant Designer in Lincoln and London, she returned to the BOV in 1962 as a scene painter, later becoming Resident Designer in both the Little Theatre and the Theatre Royal, where her most notable design was for Val May's 1965 premiere of *The Killing of Sister George,* which transferred to London and New York.

Sally Hulke, who now runs her own Bristol-based design company, SHP, had been taken to the theatre every week since she was a small child in Brighton, and always knew she wanted to be a theatre designer. A few months before starting the course at BOVTS in 1957, she offered her services at the stage door of her local theatre: 'What I didn't realise was that weekly rep in summer season at the end of a pier didn't run to an assistant for the hard-pressed designer. But I didn't even get out of the stage door again: I was given a paint brush in one hand, a bucket of whiting in the other, and told to start laying in flattage!' At the end of her first term in Bristol, Sally was invited to assist the designer on the pantomime at Lincoln Rep: 'The first thing I was asked to do was to cut out and make a very ornate coach for Cinderella, which was drawn out on hardboard. Fortunately the Bristol course combined the intellectual and academic side of design with the absolute practical needs of working in the theatre, so I'd already been taught how to use all the necessary tools.' Sally hoped to return to Lincoln as an assistant that summer, but in fact started her career there straight from BOVTS as the Resident Designer. After the customary progression from weekly rep to fortnightly and three-weekly, she moved into television when the BBC recruited twenty-four trainees (sixteen men and eight women) to service its planned expansion into a second regular channel in 1964. With eighteen years' BBC experience in London, Sally returned to Bristol in 1980 to take over the BBC design department in Whiteladies Road, returning to the Theatre School to offer practice interviews and advice to new designers.

The Head of all BOVTS Technical courses between 1955 and 1961 was former Bristol Grammar School boy Michael Ackland, who had studied design at the London Old Vic Theatre School from 1948 to 1950, then worked as an assistant designer with the famous theatre design trio known as Motley, one of whom was London Old Vic Head of Design Margaret 'Percy' Harris. Ackland's particular skill was in model making, and he stressed how important it is for designers to be able to do or make something to someone else's instructions without letting personal pride get in the way: 'My original model for John Arden's *The Happy Haven* at the Royal Court in 1960 was cut up into several pieces by George Devine at a meeting of the production staff and stuck together in a different way with sticky tape! But one must always ask "Is this better than what I have already done?" This is a lesson that is applicable to all society, and in the absence of a George Devine one has to do the cutting up of first ideas oneself.'

When Roger Jeffery replaced Michael Ackland in 1961, an arrangement was made with the BOV Company for the Resident Designer to share his skills with the School's Design students, which made available to them the wisdom and experience of the likes of Graham Barlow, Angus McPherson and John Elvery. Cyril Gates, who had worked at Glyndebourne and in weekly rep before going to the School as a Design student in 1963, was inspired by Graham Barlow's view that 'If you're going to do anything in theatre, you need to have an insight into everything'. From BOVTS, Cyril Gates had his first job with the

BOV Company, then started with the BBC as a 'holiday relief' stage manager. After working in both theatre and television for twelve years variously as a designer, stage manager/floor manager, production manager and director, he began producing TV documentaries, working his way up to Managing Editor of a range of programmes before accepting a new challenge as Head of Resources for the BBC in Manchester.

David Goldsmith, who had a passion since childhood for building model theatres, and applied to train as a designer, didn't have the required art college diploma and was accepted instead as a Stage Management student. By a happy accident - a fluke fire in the office, which destroyed the enrolment papers - he managed to attach himself to the Design course anyway, producing praiseworthy sets for both the Drama Studio and the Theatre Royal in 1962 before going into a second year as a trainee director. Wendy Shier, who was one of David Goldsmith's contemporaries on the Design course, worked for the BOV Company as a Props Mistress and returned to teach prop making part time at BOVTS. Now living in Cornwall and teaching art and drama in a school, she is actively involved with Falmouth Arts Centre - which hosts annual BOVTS West Country tours - and has designed shows for a Cornish opera company directed by Chris Warner, another early 1960s' BOVTS Technical student, who was later involved in a 1990s' scheme to develop Truro's City Hall into a multi-purpose venue to serve the whole county.

Anthony Rowe trained at BOVTS as a Technical student in the mid-1960s, and joined the BOV Company as an assistant to Graham Barlow: 'I worked in the paint shop when the Company was staging plays not only in the Theatre Royal but also at the Little Theatre in Colston Street, so we'd often be crossing the city centre with buckets of paint!' He returned to the School as Technical Assistant to Roger Jeffery, and in 1970 was invited to establish the new Design course, of which he remained Head for twenty-five years. As well as supervising the work of four Design students each year, and designing some School productions himself, he also designed productions for local operatic companies Bristol Opera and Amici, and did commercial work like television adverts with Bristol-based Aardman Animation and Christmas grottoes at Bristol Zoo: 'I enjoyed that because it's using all the same skills as you use in the theatre, but your starting point and your whole brief are different.'

Based in a tiny attic studio at Downside Road, the BOVTS Design department is run like that of a professional repertory company, and takes responsibility for developing sets and costumes for over a dozen productions between October and June, always working several weeks ahead of all the other departments. It's very demanding, but reflects the reality of a successful freelance theatre designer's working conditions, often involving two or three shows at the same time: 'You were there to put those actors in frocks and give them something to stand in front of,' laughs Annie Gosney, who went on to become Production Manager of the National's Olivier Theatre, and has returned to BOVTS as a guest designer and practice interviewer. 'How much you learned while doing it was up to you.'

'Bristol is very good at giving people the practical skills they need because every show the designers work on is seen by the paying public, so they're working for real as soon as they get to the School,' explains Anthony Rowe. 'Budgets have to balance; things have to be made and stand up and arrive on time. Actors are going to walk all over your set and wear your costumes - so it's got to work. That's a great training.'

'And a great thrill,' say many of the 1990s' students: 'Once you've experienced the buzz you get on the first night of something you've designed - there's nothing like it. It's such a good feeling - worth all the tears and the heartache beforehand,' says one.

'When we did shows at university,' adds another, 'what we saw on stage was a compromised version of the design because they didn't have the facilities or a wardrobe department. At the Theatre School there's a Wardrobe department that takes on the responsibility of producing the costumes: when I did *Love's Labour's Lost* each of the four girls in the Wardrobe made a dress for each of the four girls in the play. That was just heavenly: when they walked on to the stage, it was such a wonderful moment. And it's the same when you design a set: at the fit-up, there it is - and it does look like the model to some very large degree.'

The Head of the Design course is the only full time

member of staff supervising all the productions and available to give advice and help where necessary, for example through having established useful contacts who can supply unusual materials such as the meadow turf used in 1994 for the set of *The Romans in Britain*. But Design students also work with a variety of freelance tutors who come in to teach particular skills, offering different personal perspectives.

For many years John McMurray, who trained in theatre design at Nottingham College of Art, and was a designer at the Bristol Old Vic from 1975 until 1984, has been explaining to BOVTS students what the job of a designer actually involves, and how he approaches the process, from reading the script and discussing the production with the director, through to making costume designs, ground plans, technical drawings and a scale model of the set. Now a freelance designer for large-scale commercial conferences, he still works with trainee designers in their first term on a project that takes them through these stages.

John Elvery began teaching technical drawing to Stage Management students at the Theatre School in the 1970s: 'For stage managers and carpenters, who are on the receiving end - they're the ones who have to make or use the result - it's a matter of helping them to understand working drawings, and to get a feel for how accurate they need to be,' explains John, who took a National Diploma in Theatre Design at Wimbledon College of Art, then fulfilled an ambition to train and work as a dancer, which he did for three years before working his way up in various repertory theatres from scene painter and costume cutter to design assistant and eventually Resident Designer at Bristol Old Vic from 1972 to 1986.

The early 1990s have seen a change in the kind of students coming to BOVTS to train as designers, partly because it's almost impossible to get grants for the course. Though all have the necessary passion and ideas, and an established interest in the history of architecture, costume and theatre, not all have had basic art school training in draughtsmanship and anatomy, which led to introducing classes in technical drawing with John Elvery, and in costume drawing with BOVTS-trained Jennie Norman, who has taught set design at Bristol University Drama Department since 1984 and works as a freelance designer for companies as near as Bath's Antidote (of which she is also an

Artistic Director) and as far as Germany's Tanz Theater Wien. Among the graduates from the BOVTS Design course there are some distinguished successes and some surprising directions. Bob Crowley is undoubtedly the most illustrious theatre designer, often partnering Artistic Director Adrian Noble on productions with the RSC, and equally well-known for his work at the National and abroad. Television has attracted the talents of Beth Millward, Humphrey Jaeger, and Bryan Holgate, who worked as a designer in rep before moving into television, where his design credits include plays, star specials, drama series and sitcoms, plus two major Telethons - and thirty *Muppet Shows*. Sara Easby combines working as a freelance designer with teaching at both Bristol University Drama Department and the Theatre School. Elizabeth Bowden is an Artistic Director of Bristol-based Show of Strength, for whom she designed 1993's award-winning *A Busy Day* and the 1995 UK stage premiere of *Key Largo*. Bill Butt returned to teach prop making at BOVTS, later produced pop videos with the likes of Echo and the Bunnymen and KLF, and now runs a television and film production company called Atlas Adventures. Susannah Lipscombe co-founded a Bristol-based model making business called Cod Steaks, which has developed into a film production company and now employs nine full-time staff on projects including the art direction and sets for Nick Park's Oscar-winning animations *The Wrong Trousers* (1995) and *A Close Shave* (1996). And John Butler not only designs and makes sets and costumes but also directs, teaches, writes and acts. He still lives in Weston-super-Mare, where in the mid-1970s he co-founded a theatre company called Theatre in the Hut, for which he writes and produces local satirical pantomimes, and has also worked on many Murder Weekends, as writer, actor and producer in locations ranging from seaside hotels to the Orient Express.

In December 1995, Anthony Rowe left BOVTS to join the RSC as Design Co-ordinator: 'The work is very similar, in that I have to liaise with designers of several productions at once and make sure everything runs as smoothly as possible. But it's a new challenge, working on a much larger scale.' And with the latest new technology: the RSC is one of the few British companies to be developing computer-aided theatre design, which within five years could dispense with the need for such traditional skills as technical drawing and model making.

Since January 1996, the Design course at the BOV Theatre School has been led by Penny Fitt, former Head of Design at the Bolton Octagon, who trained with the London Old Vic's 'Percy' Harris on the postgrad Motley Theatre Design Course: 'I do have a tendency towards lopsided, grotesque and precarious structural sets,' says Penny, 'though some of them are a hundred per cent vertical and horizontal! My guiding principle is that if it's not in the text, then there's no place for it on the stage.'

18. They've got it all sewn up (and washed and ironed!): the wardrobe workers

Some of the skills required in a theatre wardrobe are highly specialised and others are extremely mundane. Students on the one year Wardrobe course at BOVTS will sometimes be making and fitting complicated corsets or crinolines, and at other times sewing endless hems or tackling a heap of washing and ironing. Wardrobe workers need people skills too, and at BOVTS they not only work closely with the designers but also get to know the actors they are kitting out in anything from a Shakespearean doublet and hose to a Humpty Dumpty outfit for *Alice Through the Looking Glass*. Sometimes they have even taken part in role-reversal exercises, performing in a short play while the Acting students take care of the clothes - a useful lesson for both in how the other side works.

Until 1981 there was no separate course at BOVTS for wardrobe, which was part of the general Technical course, with students taking turns to provide costumes for School productions. From the 1950s until the mid-1960s, costume history was taught by Bristol University lecturer Iris Brooke, a well known authority on historical costume, and by the BOV Company's Wardrobe Mistress, Alvary Williams, who used to teach cutting and making as well. The first full-time Wardrobe Mistress at the Theatre School, Vivienne Frow, was appointed in 1962. For School productions in the 1960s and 1970s, it was not practical for the Technical students to make many of the costumes, which were often hired in from London firms like Nathan's and Morris Angel's, though the School had a wonderful windfall of wardrobe stock in 1963, when the Old Vic Company was dissolved and its annexe had to be cleared: 'Several vans went up to London, and I took a pantechnicon, which we filled to the roof with everything we could lay our hands on,' recalled Roger Jeffery. 'Some of the costumes we came away with still had labels in them with "R Burton" or "L Olivier" written in the collars!' Much of this stock was to become part of the BOV Company's wardrobe hire department.

The 1960s saw a series of Wardrobe Supervisors and Assistants come and go, among them Maria Banks, Carol Baker (who married BOVTS Technical Assistant Chris Baugh), Tam Marshall and Robin Rumbelow, before the arrival of Helena Ash in 1969: 'None of the students then had come specifically to do wardrobe,' says Helena, who had no formal training but persuaded Nat Brenner that she was very handy with a sewing machine. 'It was often quite a struggle to get students to come and help get the costumes together for the productions. I used to go down to a read-through of the play, then meet and measure up the actors - who at that time were often double-cast, which meant two costumes for the same part.

'Because I had a very small budget, and the School's stock in the attic was quite limited, I spent a great deal of time searching out the cheapest sources of materials and fabrics. We were allowed to have costumes from the Bristol Old Vic Company's store, but they always gave priority to the organisations that paid, which we didn't. So I would sometimes go down and pick out what we needed to cover everybody's requirements, and then it wouldn't be there when I went back to collect it, which was very frustrating.'

All the Heads of the Wardrobe course were themselves trained at BOVTS: Jean Healey was one of Michael Ackland's Technical students in 1959-60; Franca Knight and Jill Blundell were in turn taught by her. Mrs Healey, whose father, theatre director David Phethean, directed productions for the BOV Company as well as the Theatre School, joined the staff of BOVTS in 1980 as Wardrobe Assistant to Judy Emerson, who had replaced Helena Ash in 1978. A year later, Jean Healey became Head of the new course, staying until ill health forced her to leave.

Students have described Jean Healey as 'an amazing woman - a real Mother Earth', always smiling, someone for whom nothing was too much trouble: 'She was a lovely person and an excellent teacher, always first to arrive and last to leave, and always had Radio 4 on in the background,' recalls Tracy Klyne. 'She used to invite us round to her house for tea, and we would go for day trips and have really funny outings.'

'When Jean died in 1990, I felt as though I had lost a guardian angel,' writes India Smith, who stayed a second year at BOVTS on the Design course, and has been constantly employed as a designer since she left. 'I still find her inspiring. I've never met anyone who had her joie de vivre, who worked so hard, who had such patience. She had absolute faith in me and told me I could do it even when I was making a dog's dinner of a job. When you're in such an insecure profession that means so much.'

Franca Knight, who was Head of Wardrobe from 1990 to 1992, had worked as a dresser at the London Old Vic before coming to BOVTS, from where she went to work for Angel's, then in the West End, in rep and on tour before returning to Bristol as Jean Healey's assistant in 1989. Jill Blundell, who became Head of Wardrobe in 1992, had taken a degree course in Fashion at Liverpool Polytechnic, then found her enthusiasm aroused by working voluntarily with a small theatre company - 'making costumes out of sheets and suchlike'. After training at BOVTS, she worked first at Oldham Coliseum, then for TVS in Southampton until she returned to Bristol.

Jill approaches the course in very much the same way as Jean Healey: 'Techniques haven't really changed. Jean taught us to do everything properly, cutting, marking with chalk, sewing. We were taught to do everything very well, even though it was being made for the stage, where it would only be seen from far away, and you might even be breaking it down to look old or well-worn. She believed you had to know how to make things properly first before taking the short cuts, like using flaps instead of pockets, or putting in hidden zips or velcro for quick changes in a period costume that should have hooks and bars.'

It's very much a matter of learning by doing, as much of the Wardrobe students' work is determined by the choice and pressures of School productions, though they do spend most of their first six weeks in the classroom - often alongside the Design students - learning the basics of making, fitting, hiring and maintaining the essentials of wardrobe from Jill and visiting teachers with a wide variety of experience. From the BBC, Maggie Chappelhow teaches costume history, and Jan Nethercot demonstrates basic make-up techniques, ageing and how to look after wigs and facial hair. Former BOV Wardrobe Supervisor

Jennie Falconer gives instruction in pattern cutting. Ex-students returning to share their skills include Jane Stuart-Brown for millinery ('making a hat from a block, moulding the base and creating something on top'), and Jenny Reeves on dyeing, printing and 'breaking down' techniques.

Basic cutting is based on the wardrobe workers' Bible - Janet Arnold's *Patterns of Fashion* - in which real historical costumes have been analysed to be re-created: 'We might cut the pattern out in calico, put it on the stand, then adjust it to fit the actress. Or sometimes, we cut the calico on the stand, referring directly to a design to put in the panels and the sleeves,' says Jill Blundell. Students say they can now look at a picture of any costume and feel confident that that they could make it. Janet Arnold herself was a guest teacher at the School in the 1980s.

Corsets may also be made from paper patterns or cut directly on the stand, but however it's done 'it has to be a perfect fit for the actress,' explains Sue Crawshaw, who originally came to Bristol on a work placement during a three year HND course in Theatre Wardrobe at Liverpool's City College, was a BOV Company Wardrobe Assistant and Ladies' Cutter for four years, and held the fort at BOVTS for two terms in 1995 while Jill Blundell was on maternity leave. 'A corset is supposed to be about an inch and a half too small, otherwise it doesn't do anything and you might as well not wear it. The shaping is very different - with bones and darts in different places - for different periods, and it has to be meticulously made or it doesn't work, or can even do damage. If it pulls in the wrong place on the ribs, the wearer will faint, as Edwardian ladies were wont to do!'

The Wardrobe course accepts four students a year, and requires no formal qualifications, only a basic knowledge of sewing, a passion for the theatre, and a willingness to work very, very hard for very, very long hours, often to very tight deadlines. Some come straight from school; a few are changing career after working in other fields; others have studied fashion or textiles at college, or have university degrees in subjects as diverse as Drama and Physics.

George Runcie, the only man who has ever taken the course (and, incidentally, the only Wardrobe student to get an LEA grant since 1992), had designed and made costumes for amateur productions and done a bit of fashion work before applying to BOVTS: 'I'd done a course in librarianship, but I really wanted to do something exciting and interesting where every day I would be doing something different. And I wanted to train hands-on at a professional working level. Some of the things I used to take so long over and do so badly, now I can just whiz them off - like trousers, and tunics, I've made quite a lot of those this year! We've learned a lot, it's not been like being in a classroom with a teacher. It's been more like five friends stuck in a room together being completely mad and trying to get everything finished for deadlines, working furiously till three o'clock in the morning. It's been so much fun, not a chore at all.'

'It's like a very busy rep theatre,' says Franca Knight, who now works mainly in film and TV as a costume design assistant. 'If you go from Bristol into a job as a Wardrobe Assistant, you probably won't ever work quite as hard as you did here, where you've done the tricky actors, the tricky directors, and the designers that don't understand how to make things, so you won't be fazed by anything.'

The second term is the hardest, with four or five different shows going on at the same time: 'We had to make, hire or buy all the costumes, and each of us was Wardrobe Supervisor for one production. When the first show went up, we were straight into making costumes for the next one during the day, while working as dressers at the theatre in the evenings. It got more difficult, because the first show ran over time. We had been working nine-thirty to five-thirty, but it got later and later, until we were often working from nine in the morning till ten or eleven at night, and weekends as well.'

Somehow, work experience beyond the School is also fitted in: 'They all spend some time in the Wardrobe department of the Bristol Old Vic, and we try to send them to other theatres, and to television - we've had contacts with BBC's *Casualty* - or films if there's anything going on in the area,' says Jill Blundell. 'They not only see how other organisations work, but also make useful contacts for the future. And we have a wide network of ex-students in the business, such as Nicky Burford and Jane Stoner who often need help on big touring shows.'

Several BOVTS Wardrobe graduates later worked for the BOV Company, among them former Wardrobe Mistress Clare Bredin, Wardrobe Assistant Barbara Edwards, fabric printer Jenny Reeves and, on wardrobe maintenance, Christine Lowe and Maggie Bridgett: 'My most vivid student memory was two weeks in the summer at the Minack Theatre where our performances paid for new dressing rooms (still there) instead of the cave we had to use,' writes Maggie, who became a freelance dressmaker. 'On the first day we had a terrible thunderstorm and the costumes hanging in the cave were drenched - not funny as they were heavy Elizabethan dresses and tunics. We had no drying facilities within reach, but fortunately it was hot for the first dress rehearsal and although we had a few complaints everyone wore their costume until it dried.' Other Bristol-trained wardrobe workers have sewn and supervised, hired and ironed for theatres ranging from regional rep and small-scale touring to the RSC and the Welsh National Opera, as well as for television and films.

Janet Davies originally auditioned as an actress to get into the Theatre School in 1952, but was drawn towards costume making and left at the end of her first year when offered a job as Wardrobe Supervisor with the Midland Theatre Company. She has stayed in the wardrobe ever since, working for many years with the BBC, and since 1990 for Bristol Costume Services, as well as teaching pattern cutting and millinery at BOVTS for eighteen years altogether. In the 1970s, and again in the 1980s, she used to do a two-day double act with Ian Adley (who was a colleague both at the BBC and at Rose Bruford) explaining to BOVTS students what was involved in their jobs as a designer and costume maker at the BBC.

Tracy Klyne, who stayed a second year on the School's Design course, went from BOVTS to the Royal Court as Acting Wardrobe Mistress, which within a few months led indirectly to her designing the costumes for a Steven Berkoff production. She has done freelance costume design work for television, film and the National Theatre, between working for the RSC as Wardrobe Mistress at The Pit in The Barbican, where BOVTS-trained Amanda Brown was her Deputy.

'The thing about the Bristol course is that it gives you such a broad spectrum,' says freelance costume maker Pam Vale. 'We could only learn the absolute basics, because we had so little time. But we left knowing an awful lot, even if it's a bit of everything rather than a lot of any one thing.'

19. Stage directions

As early as 1957, the Bristol Old Vic Theatre School was offering some structured training for would-be theatre directors. Duncan Ross set up a two-year course for 'producers' on which one or two students followed the Acting course for the first year, then in the second year had opportunities to direct student productions 'under the supervision of a member of the staff'. They also had one term's study of the technical aspects of staging productions, and special instruction in the preparation of scripts, rehearsal methods, and the handling of actors.

Among the earliest student directors were Jane Howell, Brian Bell, and George Roman: 'The only Directors' course available in England at the time was at the Bristol Old Vic Theatre School,' recalls Mr Roman, who went on to become the first Artistic Director at both Billingham Forum and Theatr Clwyd, and has lectured in Drama at the Universities of Swansea, Cambridge and Exeter - where he was also Artistic Director of the Northcott Theatre from 1986 to 1991. 'Although already the possessor of a pretty fair degree in Directing from the Hungarian Theatre and Film Academy, I soon became aware of the huge areas of theatrical craft and skill which my romantically talent-oriented Hungarian initiation into the profession completely disregarded: from voice production to stage lighting, from budgeting to publicity. Duncan Ross also taught me the structured preparation of a play, based on graft and academic research, as a means of liberating me as a director to use inspiration and imagination with a purpose.'

At the time, Mr Roman was also struggling to use the English language, with some amusing results. He had cast Chris Tranchell in a leading role in Julius Hay's play *My Own:* 'At one stage I gave him the instruction, "When you get here, twinkle!" He did his utmost to shine, he projected for all he was worth, but I was never satisfied and insisted that he should just "twinkle". Finally, after many tries, I said "No, no, no. When you get here, just twinkle, like this". And I winked. Nobody let on that my

English was still less than competent, which speaks of the self-restraint and kind-heartedness of everybody present.'

Brian Bell became Director of the Byre Theatre, St Andrews in the early 1960s before returning to New Zealand, where he made a successful career in television. Jane Howell had graduated from Bristol University Drama Department before joining the Producers' course at BOVTS, where her most notable achievement was a student production of *The Sport Of My Mad Mother* in the spring of 1960, which brought the School its first invitation to perform in London, at the Royal Court and Hampstead Theatre Club. It was a play well suited to the School's young performers and team-based approach: hailed by Kenneth Tynan in 1958 as representative of the best contemporary work in the theatre, it focuses on teenagers and features jazz rhythms with the characters moving in a choreographic pattern towards the climax. Playwright Ann Jellicoe had been invited to the University Drama Studio to see the School's production, and was afterwards quoted in the *Bristol Evening Post* as saying 'Much as I hate to admit it, Miss Howell's production is better than mine at the Royal Court'. She then generously invited the company to take the play to London, where *The Stage* praised the players' 'freedom and authority brought about by intensive rehearsal and astonishing rapport' and *The Observer* declared that 'the real success of the evening was as a beautifully integrated whole, which reflects the greatest credit on the Bristol Old Vic Theatre School'. Jane Howell went on to make a very successful career as a director in the theatre and on television, and was back at the Royal Court in November 1995 with another new play, *Bruises* by Judy Upton, featuring BOVTS-trained Patricia Brake in the cast.

After a year as a Design student, David Goldsmith stayed on as one of four student directors on an ambitious but ill-fated scheme set up by John Hodgson in 1962. Although the course was abandoned after two terms, when Nat Brenner replaced Richard Ainley, it did give David a useful introduction to television by allowing him to shadow the production of a weekly pop programme made at the BBC studios. By chance he had met Joan Littlewood at Christmas, and began his career with her Theatre Workshop in London's East End, where 'being a part of *Oh What A Lovely War* was one hell of a way to start in the theatre'.

It was six years before Nat countenanced another Directors' course, explaining in some mid-1960s' prospectuses that the School 'is obliged to recognise that a potential director is unable to demonstrate his promise in the manner open to an Acting student at the end of his course, i.e. by audition or by performance in School productions, and the School is reluctant to offer up groups of student actors to student producers. It is obvious that no responsible professional theatre management or organisation would entrust the direction of a play to one who has had no actual professional producing experience and yet it is equally obvious that a few directors have managed to emerge each year. In general they were either proven and excellent stage managers, or actors of authority who earned their opportunities. We advise any young man or woman who earnestly wishes to become a director to undertake the Combined Course or the Technical Course and then seek professional experience as an actor or stage manager.'

Though there was no official course, the School was still willing to help students who showed interest and promise. Chris Smith, who had done the one year Technical course in 1966-67 stayed on for a second year as a trainee director, but spent most of his time away from the School, mainly at the University and the King Square Arts Centre, and left early. After introducing the three year Acting course in 1969, Nat reorganised the Technical courses to include provision for would-be directors to stay on and work 'with the Acting students of the School on selected production exercises, and be admitted to the work of the Bristol Old Vic Company'.

In the mid-1970s BOVTS was the only drama school offering students an opportunity to direct plays for a year, with the benefit of advice. Still mindful of the problems that might arise through having student directors teaching student actors, Nat also occasionally hired half a dozen experienced professional actors - 'of the calibre of Denis Carey, Yvonne Coulette and John Franklyn-Robbins' - to work with the novice directors, among them Chris James, who came to BOVTS as a student in 1976, then stayed for two more years teaching actors and directing plays; Conor O'Malley (son of Mary O'Malley, not the playwright but the founder of Belfast's Lyric Theatre);

and Bristol University Music graduate Christopher de Souza, who went on to direct opera and to broadcast on Radio 3.

'Nat and Rudi had an extraordinary knowledge of the theatre and the world,' says Chris James, who later took an MA in Film, returned to Bristol in 1984 to found Watershed Television, and focused mainly on directing videos and commercials. 'They were discussing the policy of the School one day, whether it should follow Lee Strasberg's American Method, or Stanislavski or Brecht or whatever; and Rudi said "You know, I was talking to Helene Weigel some years ago, and she was saying 'When Bertolt Brecht was a young man, he was terribly hot-headed. And he would say these things about the Method acting and Stanislavski, but you know as he grew older ...'" And I suddenly realised that I was in an environment with people to whom Michel Saint-Denis and Bertolt Brecht were not just names you read about in books, they were real people, people who made theatre shows! You felt you were tapping into an extraordinary heritage.'

Chris Denys still brings in some professional actors for directors to practise on, but since he has been Principal, training for directors at BOVTS has been offered as an 'attachment' rather than a 'course' and is not advertised. Would-be directors with previous relevant experience may be invited to be 'generally and responsibly involved in the preparation of the School's public and in-School productions', with opportunities to attend classes on the Acting and Technical courses, to assist the professional directors and to produce their own lunchtime shows, choosing the play and the cast themselves. The average number of these 'attached' directors is four each year, and several have returned as professionals to direct public productions for the School, among them Anne Adamson, Vanessa Dodd, Bonnie Hurren and Jeremy Meadow.

With a background as a portrait painter, a language teacher and a dancer, Anne Adamson decided to become a theatre director because 'it pulled together my interest in movement, visuals and text'. After the Attachment at BOVTS, she has taught at LAMDA and directed in Bristol for the Music Box Opera Group, and her own company Out To Lunch.

Bonnie Hurren trained at RADA as an actress, and had been based in Bristol for several years before taking the

Directors' Attachment at the Theatre School: 'Most of the directors I had worked for as an actress were men,' says Bonnie, one of the founding members and regular performers with acclaimed Bristol pub theatre company Show of Strength, 'and I thought, as a woman, I would have something different to offer. Going to the Theatre School seemed a very practical way to make the transition, especially to widen my appreciation of the technical aspects.'

'Being part of a major drama school enabled me to fill in the gaps in my own knowledge and experience, but it was also a very helpful springboard into the profession,' says Jeremy Meadow, who read English at university and worked as a teacher and a stage manager before going to BOVTS, from where he went straight into a job for Charles Vance. 'He'd come to Bristol "shopping" for an Assistant Director and I worked for him for about a year, during which I was promoted to Associate Director, before going freelance.'

Adam Edsall, who went from BOVTS to Swanage to direct two plays in a ten-week summer season, had acted while studying English and Philosophy at university then worked for two years in London as a freelance director, an assistant director and on his own shows: 'I wasn't really progressing very far, I found that on the Fringe you get trapped because you can't move up into rep, and you can't move from Assistant to Director. And I thought that as actors have to train for three years, it was only fair that I should train too.'

Sabine Bauer, whose first job on leaving BOVTS was Assistant Director with Oxford Touring Company, describes her experience on the Attachment as 'like bringing a shopping trolley and taking whatever you can'. Trainee directors can meet regularly with Chris Denys to discuss the administrative and financial side of running a theatre, how to compile a season, for example, or how to check out what your audience will come to see; they can watch other directors as an assistant, learning just as much by agreeing as by disagreeing with them; and they can gain an insight into the techniques involved in all aspects of creating theatre: 'It's all very well being able to see that something's wrong but much easier to offer constructive criticism if you have learnt the language of the actor,' says one. 'Then you can say in three words what otherwise takes you half a morning to explain.'

While on the Directors' Attachment Timothy Sheader (who became an Assistant Director at the Orange Tree Theatre in Richmond within months of leaving BOVTS) took the opportunity to work as ASM and DSM on shows, finding out first hand what it feels like to be on the receiving end of a director's instructions - and that some of the things stage management do are not as simple as they look.

People have followed a wide variety of paths after the Directors' Attachment at Bristol. Henrik Ahnborg runs a state sponsored theatre company in Sweden. Nick Bamford, who was already established as a television director, formed his own F-O-D Theatre company, based in the Forest of Dean, touring small-scale ensemble productions of the classics around Gloucestershire. David Massarella was Assistant Director at Salisbury Playhouse to Artistic Director Deborah Paige, his contemporary at Bristol and now Artistic Director in Sheffield. James Runcie (son of the former Archbishop of Canterbury) is a documentary film-maker. Oxford University graduate Tim Luscombe has worked in the West End, in Chichester and in America. Neil Bartlett, who became Artistic Director of the Lyric Theatre Hammersmith in 1994, is also a writer of books and of plays produced at the National Theatre and on television, and by his own company Gloria, who performed his *Sarrasine* and *Night After Night* (in which he also appeared) at Bristol's Arnolfini, and visited the BOV's New Vic Studio in May 1996 with his 'intimate musical' *Lady Into Fox.*

A significant number of Bristol-trained actors have later made their mark as directors. John David was one, the only BOVTS graduate (so far) to become Artistic Director of the BOV Company. Alan Dossor was another: he was Artistic Director at the Liverpool Everyman from 1970-75, directed the stage premieres and subsequent West End productions of *Funny Peculiar* and Willy Russell's *John, Paul, George, Ringo and Bert* and *Breezeblock Park,* won an Emmy for a 1990 BBC TV film *First and Last* (featuring BOVTS-trained Pat Heywood and Patricia Routledge) and later directed three series of TV's *Between the Lines.* Others include international opera director Robert Carsen (who returned to the Bristol Old Vic in 1990 to direct *Lady Windermere's Fan,* with Maggie Steed as Mrs

Erlynne), Christopher Selbie in America, Robin Phillips in Canada and John Bell in Australia. Antony Tuckey, who worked as an ASM, actor (and in the late 1960s Associate Director) with the BOV Company, has been Artistic Director at the Wolsey Theatre, Ipswich since 1979; Christopher Dunham has been Artistic Director of the Palace Theatre, Westcliff since 1975. Robin Herford, who has appeared in the original productions of more Ayckbourn plays than any other actor, was an Associate Director of Scarborough's Stephen Joseph Theatre in 1979, and its Artistic Director in 1986-88 when Alan Ayckbourn went to the National Theatre for two years.

'It was actually the experience of working under a very poor director that made me realise that I should be directing and not acting,' says John Caird, who was fired from his first job as a rep actor after about four months, 'largely, I think, because I kept having ideas, and I was no naive that I didn't realise they weren't being welcomed. I was told in no uncertain terms by the person who fired me that there was no room for people like me in the professional theatre'. En route to joining the RSC, where he was an acclaimed director in the 1980s, and has been an Honorary Associate Director since 1990, John Caird worked for two years as a DSM in Jane Howell's company at Exeter Northcott ('in rehearsal and on the book in shows, really learning the craft of theatre in a practical, professional place'), then as a flyman in London's New Theatre (now the Albery), and as an Associate Director at the Manchester Contact Theatre. Working freelance after twelve years with the RSC, he viewed directing as 'a peculiar craft because it isn't a strictly necessary component of the theatre: if you were to take away one by one all the things you need to do theatre, the director would be one of the first to go. You must have audiences, and actors, and plays and playwrights, and stage management. But you can do it without a director. And any director who loses sight of that fact can be a problem: directors should have a due sense of their own ultimate irrelevance! So it's of enormous value to have been schooled in one of the important aspects, be it writing or acting, so you have a first hand experience of what it's like at the cutting edge of the most important relationships in the theatre: between actors and audience; or between playwright and actor.'

'I felt that I needed to be able to understand the craft of

acting in order to understand the craft of directing. I can understand the actor's problems from an actor's point of view,' says Greg Doran, who already had his own company, The Poor Players, before he went to the Theatre School, where he directed most of his fellow Acting students in an extra-curricular Elizabethan play, *The Book of Sir Thomas More,* which they performed at London's Young Vic, and in a version of *The Winter's Tale*, which they literally 'barnstormed' all around the West Country - in barns!

Antony Tuckey adds a note of caution: 'Sometimes if you've been an actor, you can be too soft as a director because you understand the problems.'

Sean Aita was an actor for ten years, including work with the Royal National Theatre and touring with Vienna's English Theatre, before starting to direct shows as well: 'Because I'd been doing a lot of commercial work as an actor in the theatre, I wanted to free myself up creatively, by doing some more off-the-wall work on the Fringe as a director rather than an actor, because actors on the Fringe are often at the mercy of people who've come straight out of Oxbridge and have no experience and no idea of how to treat you. So I set up a company called Secret Theatre with Adam Henderson, who was also at Bristol Old Vic Theatre School, and we presented some shows together. Then through Paul Elliott of E&B, who I'd worked for in the West End musical *Buddy,* I had a chance to learn about how pantomimes were put together, and then direct them.' While an Associate Director of the Vienna Theatre, Sean kept his work diary full by also acting, writing and teaching.

After supplementing the foundation of her two year Acting course at BOVTS with an eclectic range of theatre and therapeutic training and experience, Veronica Needa developed particular interests in working for children, community theatre and cross-cultural bridging. As Director of London Playback Theatre, a form of improvisational theatre which borders therapy, she worked with actors and musicians who invite members of the audience to tell events from their real lives and then watch them enacted on the spot. And as Director of Yellow Earth Theatre, a co-operative of British Oriental theatre practitioners integrating Eastern and Western theatre styles, she was involved in several productions since the company began in

1993, including *Moonchant,* which she co-devised and co-directed with David Tse and members of the Manchester and Liverpool Chinese communities for the 1994 City of Drama Festival.

Sonia Fraser joined the BOV Company as an ASM after leaving the School herself in 1955, and worked as both an actor and dancer for many years before 'crossing the bridge into becoming a director' in the early 1980s: 'I wanted to do it much earlier, but in those days all theatre directors were men, who all seemed to have university degrees, and women - especially actresses - would not have been considered.'

One glorious exception to this was Joan Knight, who trained at Bristol Old Vic Theatre School for two years in the early 1950s, was Artistic Director at Farnham in the early 1960s and, having retired in 1993 after twenty-five years as Artistic Director of Perth Rep, continues working as a freelance director.

20. Where do they go from here?

Anywhere and everywhere! Not just in the theatre or other areas of the performance and presentation industry, but also in a range of apparently unrelated occupations where a Theatre School training proved to be an invaluable preparation for Life: 'Both the Theatre and the Church demand self-discipline, team work, and the generous application of one's gifts to make inspiration a shared revelatory experience,' says Rev. Canon Collins - formerly BOVTS Technical student Stella Reid - who was priested in 1994 and has worked for many years in Salisbury, first as a Stage Manager at the Playhouse, then as a Canon of the Cathedral.

'It would be inaccurate to regard those who never became famous as any kind of failure,' says Brian Austin, who worked as an actor ('Simon Cord') for several years, and later established himself as a genealogist and local historian in his home town of Weston-super-Mare. 'In my own field I am one of the best at what I do, and there are several Vic School reasons for that - voice, clarity, projection, personality marketing.'

'I had no training as a businessman, but I can sell,' says Robert Crewdson, who acted in rep, film, TV and musical tours for over twenty years before moving into the fine art retail trade. 'You do it instinctively as an actor - you spend your life trying to get people to like you! And once you've sold yourself, you're more than halfway to selling the goods.'

Between acting jobs, Frankie Jordan temped as an on-site sales negotiator with a building firm: 'It's exactly like being with a film unit,' she says. 'The builders are the crew, the management are director and producers, and I'm performing for the customers - my audience.'

'The BOV training has been useful in many ways - on a superficial level it gave me the ability to appear to be in control of a situation,' adds Jenny Broughton, who went on to become Devon's first County Drama Librarian, a founder member and later Chairman of Exeter Arts Council and, since 1984, a

Magistrate on the Exeter Bench. 'The voice training has been useful throughout my working life - it comes in handy in court too! But on a deeper level I think the Theatre School trained me to really think about what makes people tick, and to empathise with all kinds of people.'

This interest in other people's character and motivation has led several BOVTS-trained actors to go into the law, mostly as probation officers or solicitors. After five years as an actor, Leslie Perrin re-trained as a solicitor but still appears on the Bristol Theatre Royal stage every year - as Managing Partner of city lawyers Osborne Clarke at their AGM. He attributes his success in his new profession partly to his actor's training: 'The biggest problem many solicitors have is that they want to tell people the answer before they've heard the question. They don't listen, so they can come across as arrogant and uncaring, even if they're not. Actors develop a sensitivity towards their audience, they not only listen but are always aware of the effect that they're creating.'

'If one avoids too much flamboyance, the experience of being a professional actor can be of immense value in other professions,' says Mark Brackenbury, who combines acting with stockbroking. 'A good actor has to know exactly the effect he is having on his audience - so has a stockbroker trying to persuade a doubtful client to make an important investment decision. An actor must be able to time a laugh line - an invaluable asset at board meetings, making presentations, or at all sorts of times. An actor should be audible without being noisy: at meetings this means that your point is always understood without antagonising anyone unnecessarily.'

'I'd always been a Production Manager, which is not dissimilar to being a Managing Director. It's still a question of getting the right people and the right things in the right place at the right time,' says Brian Croft, who trained as a stage manager at BOVTS and became Managing Director of Vari-Lite (Europe) after a backstage career which began with the National Youth Theatre, lots of rep, Arnold Wesker's famous Centre 42 Project, the early days of London's ICA (Institute of Contemporary Art) in 1968, and the Rolling Stones' first European production tour in 1970.

Clive Barker, who was Festivals Organiser for that

Centre 42 Project and later became a Senior Lecturer in Theatre
Studies at Warwick University, also trained as a stage manager,
but started his career as an actor, with Joan Littlewood's Theatre
Workshop: 'Since I left Bristol I have earned my living at every
job in the theatre, except scene painter. I was even a wardrobe
master!' says Clive, who has directed plays and trained actors all
over the world, setting out his teaching in *Theatre Games*
(Methuen 1978) which is still in print as a standard text book,
with translations in Japanese, Spanish and Hindi. He has also
written plays for stage and television, and contributed the entry
on Theatre in the current edition of *Encyclopaedia Britannica*.
Since 1985, he has been Joint Editor, with Simon Trussler, of
New Theatre Quarterly for Cambridge University Press.

Playwrights Peter Nichols and David Goodland both
trained as actors at BOVTS, and were later commissioned to
write plays that were premiered by the BOV Company in the
Theatre Royal: Nichols' *Born in the Gardens* in 1979 (which he
also directed); and Goodland's *Life and Death of a Buffalo
Soldier* in 1995. Other writers who trained as actors at BOVTS
include Scott Cherry, Emlyn Harris, and Duncan Gould (who
work mainly in TV and/or radio), Steven Deproost and Herb
Greer (whose work ranges from journalism to poetry), Martin
Hoyle (later theatre critic for the *Financial Times,* and Classical
and Opera man at *Time Out* magazine), Charles Duff (a theatre
and opera director, whose first book, *The Lost Summer,* is both a
biography of Frith Banbury and an entertaining account of the
heyday of the West End theatre), and Simon Shaw, author of five
criminal black comedies, who uses his theatre experience to
provide the background for hilariously ingenious murder plots
that have twice won him the Crime Writers' Last Laugh Award
for funniest book of the year.

In 1995, John Dalby published a book and cassette
called *How To Speak Well In Business*. Once described by BBC
critics as 'a cross between John Osborne and Frankie Howerd',
Bristol-born John was one of only two men in the BOV Theatre
School's first full time intake, went straight into the BOV
Company as an ASM in 1947, and in 1996 is still working as a
composer, musical director, cabaret revue performer and teacher
of voice and singing. He was most widely known in the 1960s,
when he took over the Dudley Moore role in *Beyond the Fringe*

in Bristol, the West End and on tour; and wrote the book and music for the Theatre Royal Stratford East production *The Rose and the Ring,* which in 1964 was a massive hit as the first pantomime to use the style of current pop music, then the Beatles.

The Bristol Old Vic Theatre School has always turned out versatile performers, and was particularly at good at training the kind of all-round repertory actors who were the backbone of the theatre world in the 1950s and 1960s, and even into the early 1980s, travelling from town to town, being signed up to play a variety of roles in a season of productions. Repertory theatre had taken over from the old Victorian 'stock companies' in the early years of the twentieth century. In Manchester, Liverpool, Birmingham, Bristol, and by the 1950s in over a hundred regional theatres, companies presented a 'repertoire' of plays with the same actors in the cast of at least one and sometimes more productions every week. But the new availability and affordability of television greatly reduced the regular audience until by 1960 there were only forty-four regional reps still working. Not only were there fewer theatres, there were also fewer productions, as weekly and fortnightly rep gave way to putting on one play every three or four weeks.

At their best, the reps provided a very practical starting point for young actors, who were often signed up for as long as forty weeks on an 'Esher Standard Contract' with a 'do-anything' clause. Having to rehearse for one play during the day, perform in another in the evening and learn lines for a third that was coming soon helped to develop discipline, memory, versatility and resourcefulness: 'You'd go to a rep and play a hundred and one parts - a lot that you weren't right for, but it was facing an audience eight times a week. That was really a continuation of the training,' says Richard Frost. 'Young actors don't get that now, that constant exposure to audiences and rehearsals and different directors.'

'Until the 1980s, most actors took it for granted that they would begin their working life in one of the regional theatres,' says Chris Denys. 'But over the last ten years, very few have had the opportunity of a thirty-week contract to a theatre company where they're working on a series of different projects with people who've been in the business thirty years. It wasn't until 1991 that I accepted for the first time that a graduate could be "off my conscience" with a first job in television - until then I always expected to launch them through the theatre.'

Looking to the future - the recent Broadcasting Bills, the ITV franchise-auctions, the privatisation of large parts of the BBC, the growth of independent producers, cable, satellite, CD-ROM - these things have already altered the profession out of all recognition - and then there's whatever lies around the next corner. The School regards all these changes as new opportunities for which students must be prepared during their training. Cameras are now increasingly, though carefully, introduced into more and more first-year classwork but it is still the theatre - in spite of all its current difficulties - with which the School is most concerned.

Chris Denys refuses to subscribe to the prevailing pessimistic view: 'Certainly we have to provide people with life-support systems - to produce survivors. There are few enough safety nets these days and who knows if society will provide any at all in the future? It has always been the case that the people who most subsidise the theatre are those who work in it but they can only do so if they are able to make a living as the foundation for survival.

'I still passionately believe in the concept of our National Theatre as being more than just two large companies, however admirable, but being a grid - an octopus if you like - of building-based and touring companies covering the nation and making a wide range of theatre of all kinds and styles available for everybody - wherever they live and however little they can afford to pay. In present circumstances, that looks like a pretty ridiculous dream but I firmly believe that times change for the better as well as the worse and that, if we keep pestering and bullying successive governments, we can not only restore what we had but build it to be stronger and more comprehensive.

'We can only do that though if, here and now, we create a pool of highly motivated, highly skilled, highly versatile and adaptable, hugely talented, and passionately committed people.'

Acknowledgements

Grateful thanks to all the people who gave their time to write or talk to the author and helped make this book possible:

Research carried out between autumn 1993 and spring 1996 identified 2,288 sometime students at the Bristol Old Vic Theatre School between 1946 and 1996, located 1,156 and established contact with 470 of them. Other people who shared their memories and opinions all had a direct personal involvement with the School. These lists are in alphabetical order of professional or current surname, with brackets indicating alternative names by which people have been known.

Students: Gavin Abbott, Janey Adams, Anne Adamson, Henrik Ahnborg, Sean Aita, Eugene Ambrose, Simeon Andrews, Pat Armstrong, Tom Ashcroft, Christopher Ashley, Brian Austin (Simon Cord), Joe Aveline, Richard Bacon, Peter Bailey, Peter Baldwin, Ashley Bale, Nick Bamford, Nichola Barber, Clive Barker, Tim Barker, Tim Barlow, Gaynor Barrett, Gillian Barrington, James Barriscale, Neil Bartlett, Rodger Barton, Emma Battcock, Sabine Bauer, Mark Beardsmore, Maria-Theresa Bechaalani, Bernard Behrens, Timothy Bentinck, Simon Beresford, Neil Bett, Christopher Biggins, Peter Birrel, Roger Bizley, Patrick Blackwell, Nicholas Blane, Caroline Bliss, Rachel Blues, Julien Boast, Eamon Boland, Sam Bond, Samantha Bond, Jonathan Bonner, Kathryn Bools, Dominic Borrelli, Lisa Bowerman, Robin Bowerman, Elizabeth Bowden, Simon Bowles, William Boyde (Thompson), Mark Brackenbury, Virginia Brackenbury (Stott), Cathryn Bradshaw, Michelle (Marian) Braidman, Patricia Brake, Christopher Bramwell, Joanna Branch, Jill Brassington, Sam Breckman, Roger (David) Brierley, Lucy Briers, Jenny Broughton (Mollan), Amanda Brown, Gerard Brown, Dominic Brunt, Mark Buffery, Nicky Burford, Camilla Burgess (Lumsden), Sophie Burrows, John Butler, John Caird, Ruth Caleb, Saul Cambridge, Teresa Campbell, Selena Carey-Jones, Anji Carroll, Robert Carsen, Julian Chaloner, Julian Checkley, Scott Cherry, Jeremy Child, Philip Childs, David Chivers, Hazel (Rachael) Clyne, Amanda Cole, Diane Collett (Smith), Rebecca Collett, Charlotte Collingwood, Alan Collins, Stella Collins (Reid), Shane Connaughton, Mike Cooper (Quentin), Kenneth Cope, Allan Corduner, Peter Coryndon, Julian Courtenay (Pinfield), Alex Cox, Vivienne Cozens, David Craik, Robert Crewdson, Brian Croft, Annette Crosbie, Suzan Crowley, Michael Culkin, Jocelyn Cunningham, Gary Curran, John Dalby, John David (Baker), Nicholas David (Bayley), Gwenllian Davies (Ann Norman), Jessie Davis, Gary Davy, Catherine de Goris, Giovanni Del Vecchio, Steven Deproost, Stephen Dillane (Dillon), Jonathan Dockar-Drysdale, Jo Dodds, Christopher Donnelly,

Greg Doran, Alan Dossor, Vernon Douglas, Susan Dowdall, Wayne Dowdeswell, Simon Drew, Danny Dryer, Charles Duff, Christopher Dunham, Heidi Easton, Gillian Eaton (Morgan), Patricia Eddington (Scott), Adam Edsall, Allan Edwards, Rob Edwards, William Eedle, Sandor Elès, James Ellis, Jennifer Ellis (Harrison), Michael Ellison, Clare England, Susie England (Riches), Edward Evanko, Angela Fairclough, Anthony Falkingham, Rachel Fielding (Bell), Gudmunder Finnsson, Richard Fleming, Julia Ford, David Forrester, Neal Foster, Vincent Franklin, Sonia Fraser, David Frederickson (Skinner), Ian Frost, Richard Frost, Christopher Fry, James (Craig) Gaddas, Roger Gage, Damian Gaskin, Cyril Gates, Derek Gay, Emma Gerrish, Martin Scott Gilmore, David Goldsmith, Sophie Goodchild, David Goodland, Duncan Gould, John Grantham, Stephen Gray, Helen Green, Poppy Green (Candida Fawsitt), Herb Greer, Jeffrey Grenfell-Hill, Katherine Grice, Emily Grimes, Christopher Grimes, Christopher Hadfield, Michael Hadley, Gilbert Halcrow, Brad Hall, Jean Hampson (Grigg), Allison Hancock, Peter Handley, Bob Harris, Emlyn Harris, Rachel Hartland, Jonathan Hartman, Charlotte Harvey, Ross Harvey, Leader Hawkins, Catherine Hayes-Davies (Fluff Browne), Carole Hayman, Prue Haynes, Pippa (Philippa) Haywood, Patricia Healey, Adam Henderson, Robin Herford, Matthew Hewitt, Pat Heywood, Kim Hicks, Maggie Higgins, Daniel Hill, Tom Goodman Hill, Simon Hirst, Robin Hodson, Lisa Hoghton (Sibley), Glenn Holderness, Bryan Holgate, Lisa Hollander, Sarah-Jane Holm, Robert Holmes, Jane Howell, Tony Howes, Martin Hoyle, Mark Hubbard, Sally Hulke, Jeremy Irons, Humphrey Jaeger, Ian G James, Milton Johns (John Milton), Aled Jones, Frankie Jordan, Shauna Kanter, Rashid Karapiet, Eve Karpf, Marian Kemmer, Jacqueline King, Vicky King, Jacqueline Kington, Jack Klaff, Tracy Klyne, Joan Knight, Penny Krinski, Mark Lambert, Clare Lambert-Wilson, Robert Lang, Angela Langfield, Guy Lankester, Jane Lapotaire, Phyllida Law, Pip Lawrence, Peter Layton (Thomas), Monette Lee, Barbara Leigh-Hunt, Satara Lester, Gillian Lewis, Susannah Lipscombe, Caroline Loncq, Daphne Lucas, Nick Lucas, Nicholas Lumley, Rosie Lumley, Damian Lunn, Sian Lyall, Michael Lynch, Lindsey Mack, Donalh MacNeil, Susan Majolier, Sara Markland, Amy Marston, Claire Mason, Sally Mates, Gloria de Matos, Damien Matthews, Clare McCarron, Andrea McCulloch, Rohan McCullough, John McEnery, Annie McGann (Milner), Victor McGuire, Hugh McInally, Vivienne McKee, Jeff McKenna (Jefferson Clode), Abigail McKern, Anne McMurdo, Christopher Mellows, Patrick Miller, Antony Milne (Stoughton), Joanne Mitchell, Dawn Monaghan, Carolyn Montagu, Mauro Montuschi, Alan Moore, Jacqueline Morgan (Williams), Vicki Morrison, Margaret Nagle (Bridgett), Veronica Needa, Mark Negus-Bullock, Paul Neville, Rachel Niblock, Peter Nichols, Trudi Ninnim (Cobbin), Sarah Nolte (Cowling, Phillips), Marta Nordal, Ben Oldfield, Rachael Oldfield, Karin Olebjork, Iain Osborn, Mike Ostler, Debra Overton, Graham Padden, Deborah Paige (Deborah Dunhill), Paul Panting, Luke Pascoe (Bernard Roberts), Shona Penman, Leslie Perrin, Tim Perrin, Dariel Pertwee, Robert Peters, Rob Pheby, Rachel Pierman, Tim Pigott-Smith, Sam Pine, Richard Platt, Polly Pleasence,

Louise Plowright, Sarah Porter, Graham Pountney, Robin Pratt (Lawrence), Tim Preece, Gabriel Prendergast, Gareth Tudor Price, Rupert Procter, Sarah Pugsley, Naomi Pullen, Christopher Punter, Paul Rattigan, Michael Read, Heather Redmond (Glenn), Graham Rees, Alastair Reid, Emma Reid, Graham Richards, Stella Richards, Simon Richardson, Neil Roberts, Cecily Robinson, Frederick Robinson, Jennifer Robson (Woodford), Marilla Robson, George Roman, Kim Romer, David Roper, Anna Rose, Norman Rossington, Liz Rothschild, Adam Rowntree, George Runcie, Clive Rust, Cathy Ryan, Margaret Sadler Watson, Lin Sagovsky, Adele Salem (Saleem), Ian Sanders (Sanderson), Luke Sapsed, Rob Sayer, Greta Scacchi, Jenny Seagrove, Katy Secombe, Mary Sedgewick (Chivers), Christopher Selbie, John Sharian, Michael Sharvell-Martin (Martin), Simon Shaw, David Shawyer (Scheuer), Timothy Sheader, Terry Sheppard, Geoffrey Sherman, Wendy Anne Shier (Rowley), Sue Shousha, Arthur Sibley, Anne Simensen, Clare Simmonds, Alisdair Simpson, Marc Sinden, Roy Skelton, Nikki Skinner, Julian Slade, Anne Smith, Chris Smith, India (Deborah) Smith, Victoria Smurfit, Nadine Sparshott (Ellison), Jessica Stack, Tim Stedman, Mary Steele, Rikke Steffensen, Heida Steindors (Ragnheidur Steindórsdóttir), Sévan Stephan, Clive Stevenson, Althea Stewart, Pippa Stewart-Hogg, Allan (William) Stirland, Jane Stoner, David Straun (Smith), Theresa Streatfield, Trudie Styler, Robert Swales, John Telfer, Sophie Thompson, Richard John Thomson, Magnus Geir Thordarson, John (Joachim) Tillinger, John Toogood, Susan Tordoff, Peter Townsend, Chris Tranchell, Simon Treves, Jack Tripp (John Tripp-Edwards), Antony Tuckey, Pam Vale, Rena Valeh, Jackie Vance, Diana Van Fossen, Anthony Venditti, Amanda Villamayor, Merriel Waggoner, Cecilia Waldensten, Chris Warner, Nicola (Jane) Warren, Neville Watchurst, Richard Wellings-Thomas, Lara J West, Simon West, Demelza-Dawn Westlake, Simon Westwood, Brian Wheeler, Marcia Wheeler, Gene Wilder (Jerry Silberman), Lucinda Williams (Cindy Brown), Barbara Wilshere, Mavis Winter (Luke), Bridget Wood, Jacqueline Wood (Stanbury), Valerie Wood (Newman), Jo Woodcock, Penelope Woodman, Ken Woodward, Michael Woolley, Chahine Yavroyan, Hugh Young.

Past and present staff, guest teachers and directors: Michael Ackland, Andrew Allpass, Helena Ash, George Brandt, Nat Brenner (from a 1992 BBC radio interview with the author), Lynn (Alwyn) Britt, Geoffrey Buckley, Aubrey Budd, June Burrough, Joan Cairncross, Adrian Cairns, Maggie Collins, Sue Crawshaw, Allan Daniels, Douglas Dempster, Christopher Denys, John Elvery, Lynette Erving, Mick Escott, Jennie Falconer, Colin Godman, Gail Gordon, Chris Harris, Jerry Hicks, John Hodgson, Jonathan Howell, Roger Jeffery, Elwyn Johnson, John McMurray, Nell Moody (extracts from interview reproduced with the permission of Dr Richard Thompson, The Burra Moody Archive 1996), Erika Neumann, John Oxley, Neil Rhoden, Paul Rummer, Rudi (Raphael) Shelly, Paula Spielman (Gwyn-Davies), Francis Thomas, John Waterhouse, Glynne Wickham, Cliff Zenker.

Those who have both trained and taught at BOVTS: John Bell, Jill Blundell, Jenny Bolt, Bill Butt, Brian Buttle, Stephanie Cole, Janet Davies (Wynne-Willson), Anthony Falkingham, Sonia Fraser, Annie Gosney, John Hartoch, Richard Howard, Bonnie Hurren, Chris James (Dennis), Franca Knight, Jane Lapotaire, Carol Mackenzie, Rita McKerrow, Jeremy Meadow, Simon Nicholls, Jennie Norman, Marion Reed, David Rigden, Anthony Rowe, David Henry Salter, Ruth Sidery, Carol A Smith, Jane Stuart-Brown (Brown), John Telfer, John Webb, Tim Williams.

Other contributors: Rev. Neville Boundy (Chaplain to the BOV Company and Theatre School), Richard Cottrell, James B Douglas, J Myrtle Goulden, Andrew Hay, Dave Machin, Liz Mailes (Stanley), Andrew Neil, Harold Pinter, Ray Price (Chairman, BOV Theatre Club), Marianne Ross, Susie Sibert (Brenner), Christopher Stanley, Gordon Steff, Derek Warwick, Rodney West, Peggy Ann Wood (Russell).

Thanks for supplying photographs to: Roger Brierley (15) David Chivers and Mary Sedgewick (2) Maggie Collins (12) John Dalby (3, 5 and 6) Douglas Dempster (17, 18, and 20 to 24 inclusive) Bob Harris (8, 9, 10 and 28) Peter Layton (13 and 14) Rudi Shelly (4 and 11) Christopher Stanley and Liz Mailes (7) Antony Tuckey (1) BOV Theatre School (16, 19, 25, 26, 27, and 29 to 41 inclusive).

Photographers: Derek Balmer (17, 18, 20) Peter Cook (38) Allan Daniels (16) Jonathan Dockar-Drysdale (25) Tim Edgar (32, 35) Mick Escott (26, 33, 34, 36, 39, 40, 41) Liz Fjelle (27, 29, 30, 31) Roger Gilmour (21) Bob Harris (8, 9, 10) Desmond Tripp (3, 14) Antony Tuckey (1) Bristol United Press (13, 37) Not known: 2, 4, 5, 6, 7, 11, 12, 15, 19, 22, 23, 24, 28.

Index